WHEN GOD TAKES TOO LONG

Learning to
Thrive During
Life's Delays

Joseph Bentz

BEACON HILL PRESS
OF KANSAS CITY

Copyright 2005
By Joseph Bentz and Beacon Hill Press of Kansas City

ISBN 978-0-8341-2218-5

Printed in the
United States of America

Cover Design: Chad Cherry

Library of Congress Cataloging-in-Publication Data

Bentz, Joseph, 1961-
    When God takes too long : learning to thrive during life's delays / Joseph Bentz.
        p. cm.
    Includes bibliographical references.
    ISBN 0-8341-2218-9 (pbk.)
    1. Expectation (Psychology)—Religious aspects—Christianity. 2. Waiting (Philosophy)
3. Patience—Religious aspects—Christianity. 4. Providence and government of God.
5. Trust in God. I. Title.
    BV4647.E93B46 2005
    248.8'6—dc22
                                                                    2005028539

10 9 8 7 6 5 4 3 2

To
Peggy,
who was worth the wait

CONTENTS

Invitation to the Reader   7

Introduction: Why Is God So Slow?   13

Part 1: Principles of Waiting on God

1. Principle 1: *Expect some frustrating detours if you're   21
   going to follow God.*

2. Principle 2: *Assume that God is at work—even when   30
   you don't understand what He's doing.*

3. Principle 3: *Remember your identity in God during   39
   the long days of waiting.*

4. Principle 4: *Trust God—even though you're likely to   46
   feel His way is not the best way.*

5. Principle 5: *Wait and obey—even as things seem to   52
   get worse.*

6. Principle 6: *Have faith that in His good time God will   59
   sweep away the obstacles.*

7. Principle 7: *Remind yourself of what the Lord did   66
   for you in the past.*

8. Principle 8: *Wait when it's time to wait and act   71
   when it's time to act.*

9. Principle 9: *Know your enemies—their names are   81
   Restlessness, Complaining, and Disobedience.*

10. Principle 10: *Cling to God's purposes—even if you   89
    have a quicker plan of your own.*

Part 2: Perspectives on Time and God's Timing

11. Aren't We There Yet? Coming to Grips with the   99
    Nature of Time

12. Embracing the Moment: How Not to Wait Your Life Away   112

13. Stay the Course: Mastering the Discipline of Waiting   122

14. Casting Off the Boundaries of Time: How God's Desires   137
    for Our Lives May Reach Farther Than We Ever Dreamed

15. God Has All the Time in the World—and More: 150
    An Eternal Perspective on Waiting

Notes   157

Acknowledgments   159

INVITATION TO THE READER
Learning to Thrive in the Midst of Life's Supreme Frustration

When I look at the lives of the college students I teach, it's hard not to be envious. Young, full of energy, full of endless possibilities, their lives are temporarily free of many of the responsibilities that will later bog them down. They have the opportunity to spend their days studying fascinating subjects; socializing with friends; dating; pursuing interests like sports, music, or drama; and dreaming of their plans for the future.

And yet when I recently stopped on a sunny campus sidewalk to talk to one of my top students, her first words were "Only 27 more days 'til graduation!"

Though in my eyes her circumstances were so inviting that she should want to hang on to every moment, for her, the *now* was simply an inconvenient time she had to endure long enough to get to her "real" life, which was after graduation. She rattled off a list of the tests, papers, and other stressful tasks that stood in her way of "getting this semester over."

I told her, "Someday you'll look back on your time in college and wish it hadn't gone by so fast. You'll wish you had let yourself enjoy it more."

She nodded and smiled, but I could tell she didn't believe me. The present moved too slowly for her. Life would begin when the waiting ended.

I understand how she feels. I, too, spend most of my life waiting—to get to the next break in the school calendar, to push through traffic, to inch my way toward the checkout counter, to get a phone call returned, to get my food from the waitress.

Social commentator Carl Honore writes that "the whole world is time-sick." He borrowed his definition of "time-sickness" from Larry Dorsey, who describes the condition as the obsessive belief "that time is getting away, that there isn't enough of it, and that you must pedal faster and faster to keep up."[1]

Part of our time-sickness can be dismissed as simply an inconvenient by-product of living in a fast-paced world. Our frustration builds as we waste precious time waiting for cars ahead of us to move, waiting for the traffic light to change, waiting for sites on the Internet to pop up, waiting for the mail to arrive, waiting to get through lines at the airport, waiting for the plane to stop taxiing around the runway and finally take off, waiting for the phone to ring, waiting for our prescription to be filled, waiting for the doctor to see us, waiting for the microwave to cook our food.

These are small examples of the frustration of waiting, but for a time-obsessed people, even trivial incidents like this can lead to dire consequences. Honore writes of a man in Los Angeles who started a fight in a supermarket when someone ahead of him was too slow packing his groceries, and of a woman who threatened to kill a delivery man whose truck blocked her way for a few minutes. Describing the "chronic frustration that bubbles just below the surface of modern life," he writes, "Anyone or anything that steps in our way, that slows us down, that stops us from getting exactly what we want when we want it, becomes the enemy. So the smallest setback, the slightest delay, the merest whiff of slowness, can now provoke vein-popping fury in otherwise ordinary people."[2]

As bothersome as those countless everyday incidents of waiting can be, the time-sickness I have struggled with goes even deeper and is more disturbing. One of my greatest frustrations as a Christian is that I'm always waiting on God to act. This complaint—that God is too slow—is not one I have frequently stated out loud. It sounds too disrespectful, hints too much of a lack of faith.

How many of us have felt that for no reason we can fathom, God is dangling the things that are most important to us just out of our reach? We wait, sometimes for years, for our deepest longings to be fulfilled.

Some devoted Christians get stuck in dead-end jobs even though they feel certain they could serve God in greater ways if only He would open the opportunity. Some wait for a godly spouse, some couples wait for the gift of children, some parents wait for their grown children to return to the Lord. People who have dedicated their lives to serving the Lord wait in disappointed bafflement as their work seems to yield no fruit.

Often I've watched others move forward while I'm still *waiting* for my life to happen. At a time like that, part of me senses God's distant call, remembers His promises, and wants to believe that He has ideas for my life and will fulfill His purposes if I trust and obey Him.

But another part of me believes the fulfillment will never really come, that I'm only tantalized with it, and that I'll be left discouraged, doubting, waiting. I feel on the verge of a breakthrough, but it never quite gets there.

I yearn to serve the Lord, to step forward and obey Him as did the great figures of the Bible—Abraham, Moses, David, Paul—but I'm confused, waiting for clear orders, kept at a distance by the invisible barriers of God's silence, His inaction, His dawdling pace. Why would He make me wait so long for the very things He wants for me?

Is He silent because He's not there? Does He not act because I'm not important to Him? Does this waiting have *meaning*?

As I approached this book, I decided that in order to seek answers to these questions, I first needed to read the entire Bible with the issue of *waiting* in mind. I also wanted to find out what other writers and thinkers had said about it, and I wanted to talk to fellow Christians to see what part waiting had played in their lives.

I discovered that I'm not alone in my perception that I spend much of my life waiting on God. Not only do my fellow Christians struggle with God's apparent slowness, but waiting is pervasive in the Bible as well. The Bible is full of great "waiters," such as Abraham, Moses, Joseph, Noah, David, Jeremiah, Jonah, Zechariah, Elizabeth, Paul, and others. The truth is that they spent far more years waiting on God than they did parting the sea or building an ark or giving birth to a prophet. How did they endure that frustration? What gave them the wisdom to hold out for those astonishing breakthroughs that often came only after the darkest and most discouraging periods of silence from God, after most people would already have given up on Him?

Another question I wanted to examine was "How does God's sense of time differ from ours?" When we're in the presence of a God who transcends time, what does it mean when we call His actions "fast" or "slow"? How can those terms be defined? I gaze up in amazement at a giant sequoia tree that has taken more than 3,000 years to reach its magnificent height, and yet I grow impatient waiting 30 seconds for the traffic light to change. What is fast? What is slow? What is *time*?

Again and again I see that God's ways of accomplishing His purposes are so unusual that His eccentricity becomes the norm rather than the exception. Will His timing in our lives always be unpredictable and seemingly capricious? How can we enter into the flow of God's desires for us when that stream carries us along a strange, unpredictable route?

When God makes us wait a long time, one of our biggest temptations is to abandon His slow plan and search for a shortcut. Scripture is full of people who tried to "improve" on God's timing and speed things up a bit—with devastating results. How can we avoid that trap?

In a time-obsessed culture, it's easy to get so focused on what life will be like after some future event—once I get that

promotion, once I graduate, once I get married, once I retire
—that we lose the *present* with all its richness and joy and
purpose. How can we reach toward the future that we long
for while also being passionately alive to what God is doing in
our lives right now?

As the ideas I confront in this book gradually emerged, I
was able to change my *perspective* on waiting and my *actions*
in response to it. As I alter my attitude toward waiting, I feel
released from the pressure to make everything happen faster
and to force a certain outcome. Instead of resisting God's direction or trying to replace it with a shortcut, I am learning to
trust Him with where He's taking me and how long it may
take to get there.

I'm cutting away the needless striving, the constant worry
over the future, second-guessing God, the destructive spirit of
envy and over-competition that makes me believe I need to
speed up my life to gain some elusive advantage over those
who move at a different pace. I feel freer to enjoy the moment, not ignoring the future but not sacrificing *today* for it
either.

This book is for people who have struggled with a God
who seems too slow but who still want to follow His leading
in their lives. If you've been discouraged by the fact that life is
mostly a game of waiting and you want to break the power of
that frustration in your life, then I invite you to read on.

INTRODUCTION
Why Is God So Slow?

When He seems to take forever, is He working out a plan?

I want to serve God passionately.

I don't want to spend my life focused on mere survival, going through the motions of driving back and forth to work, mowing the lawn, paying the bills, showing up at church. I want to do big things for God. I want my life as a Christian to be an adventure!

So why does God keep me waiting? *I'm ready, Lord! Ready to do great things in your name and for your glory. I'm ready to conquer armies, part seas, crumble walls to the ground. So let's go!*

I find myself envying the heroes of the Bible, all those courageous men and women of a thousand Sunday School lessons. I think of Moses standing up to Pharaoh. When he demands, "Let my people go," it isn't empty bravado, it's the command of God, backed up by the power of plagues. I see Moses standing astounded in front of that burning bush, listening to the very voice of God. I see him courageously leading the people through a desert to the Promised Land. I see him encountering God in His blazing glory on the mountain, receiving the Ten Commandments. What a joy it must have been for Moses to follow a plan from God that had such clarity, such purpose!

I see Noah leading his family and the animals into the ark. I see Abraham witnessing the astonishing birth of his son to his aged wife, a miracle that will bring about the fulfillment of God's promise of offspring that will outnumber the stars. I see David slaying Goliath. I see Gideon. I see Ruth. I see Jonah. I see Jeremiah. I see John the Baptist. Mary. Stephen. Paul. Peter.

In the meantime, I stop at the convenience store to pick up a gallon of milk. I help my kids with their homework, throw in a load of laundry, watch the news on television. I'm behind in my work. My career has not progressed as far as I had hoped. Others are getting ahead of me! The bushes need to be trimmed. Why can't I keep the weight off? What will my life be like five years from now? How much longer will I feel as if I'm running in place?

Not that life has been devoid of exciting moments. I've witnessed God act in ways that border on miraculous. I've seen Him answer prayers. I've felt the deep joy and sense of purpose of obeying His will and taking part in His Kingdom-building work that was far beyond me.

But I've known just as many times when the doors of opportunity have slammed shut. The all-important phone calls have not been returned. The possibilities for breakthrough have melted away without resolution, not even the clarity of a definitive rejection.

Why can't my life be more like the lives of those great men and women of the Bible who charged forward so confidently, overcoming unimaginable predicaments through God's awesome power?

Did I Miss Something?

It's time to step back.

Maybe I overlooked something in the stories of those biblical heroes I so admire. Is there anything in their stories that holds the clue to God's timing?

As I read through the entire Bible with that question in mind, I discovered that almost no one whose story is recorded in the Bible was spared those long stretches when he or she must have wondered what God was doing and why He was taking so long to do it. Entire nations waited on Him to act. Again and again His timing was surprising, even bizarre. Some complained loudly against His slowness and His silence. For others, however, not a word is recorded about the months, years, and decades they spent waiting on God.

By the time I finished reading the Bible, I had hundreds of pages of notes on God's timing in the Bible and the ways He uses waiting. If His treatment of people in the Bible is any indication of how He'll handle us, then many of us are in for some big surprises.

A Note on God's Plan for Me: Does He Have One?

Whenever we speak of God's plan for our lives, we Christians do so in the belief there's one overriding desire He has for each of us: salvation. At the core of our faith is the conviction that the blood of Jesus Christ covers our sins and makes us right with God. It's pointless to worry about any other desires He may have for our lives if we've not partaken in this most important plan of all time.

The way to experience God's plan of salvation is first to acknowledge that we're born sinners. Rom. 3:23 says that "all have sinned and fall short of the glory of God." God's answer to this problem of sin is Jesus Christ: "For God so loved the world that he gave his one and only Son, that whoever believes in him shall not perish but have eternal life" (John 3:16). As Randy Alcorn succinctly describes it,

> We're told that "God made him [Christ] who had no sin to be sin for us, so that in him we might become the righteousness of God" (2 Corinthians 5:21). This means that even though we are under God's wrath for our sins, Jesus died on the cross as our representative, our substitute. God then poured out his wrath on Christ instead of on us. Christ, who stood in our place, conveyed his righteousness

to us so that we are declared innocent of all our sins and declared righteous, so that we may enter the very presence of God in Heaven and be at home with him there.[1]

After His sacrificial death, Jesus rose from the grave. Because of what Christ did, God freely offers forgiveness to anyone who turns to Him in repentance: "If we confess our sins, He who is faithful and just will forgive us our sins and cleanse us from all unrighteousness" (1 John 1:9, NIB). God's plan of salvation cannot be earned, manipulated, or negotiated. We receive forgiveness as a gift.

But our journeys as Christians don't stop there. Ephesians 2:10 says, "For we are what He has made us, created in Christ Jesus for good works, which God prepared beforehand to be our way of life" (NIB). Andy Stanley, author of *Visioneering*, writes,

> Honoring God involves discovering his picture or vision of what our lives could and should be. Glorifying God involves discovering what we could and should accomplish. We were created and re-created with his purposes in mind. And until we discover his purpose—and follow through—there will always be a hole in our soul.[2]

Where does He want to take us? What does He want to do in our lives? For those who feel stuck, with their lives seemingly on hold as they wait on God to act, is there a purpose behind His peculiar methods and timing?

Coming to Terms with God's Timing

One biblical figure whose story sheds light on many aspects of God's sense of timing is Moses. Few people in history have seen God do more amazing things in their lives than he did. From the moment Moses was born, God was working miracles for him. As an infant, he was saved from slaughter and rescued by Pharaoh's daughter, of all people. What a thrill to grow up in Pharaoh's court in advance of his real work — to free his people from the bondage of slavery and lead them to the Promised Land!

From the story of Moses a number of principles about God's timing emerge, and these principles are confirmed repeatedly in the stories of biblical figures such as Joseph, Abraham, David, and others. The following chapters will examine those principles to see how they might apply to our own Christian journeys. Understanding how God worked in the lives of these other people of faith may help us come to grips with the strange ways He's working in our own lives. If God is working in your life along a predictable, smooth path, then you're the exception, not the rule. Throughout human history, He has done otherwise. Let's now take a look at some of the surprising ways in which He works.

Part 1
PRINCIPLES OF
WAITING ON GOD

One

PRINCIPLE 1

Expect some frustrating detours if you're going to follow God.

MY FRIEND JILL is one of the most committed Christians I know. But when God called her into full-time ministry, she fought Him. The call made no sense to her. She said, "I was moving up the corporate ladder when I surrendered my heart and life to Christ. I loved my career, and it gave me a sense of fulfillment. God was blessing me with the necessary skills to be successful." Why would God want her to be a pastor? She got tongue-tied whenever she had to speak in public. She had no theological background or education. She was a single woman in a denomination where female pastors were rare. Why couldn't she serve God more effectively right where she was?

She resisted the call, but she could not escape it. She prayed. She sought advice from counselors, pastors, her non-Christian boss, her parents, and anyone else who would listen. She spent weeks making excuses, but in the end she trusted God, quit her job, and started down the long path toward becoming a pastor.

Jill walked away from everything familiar and enrolled in a theology program at a Christian university. While a full-time student, she eked out a living in the only jobs available to her there, which were low-paying and outside her field. After four hard years, she earned a bachelor's degree and was uprooted again, this time to a seminary in a different state. Once again, supporting herself while going to school full-time was not easy, but she worked at it semester after semester, guided by her call.

By the time she had finished her seminary degree, Jill had spent the better part of a decade pursuing her goal. She had worked twice as hard as before, had accepted a lower standard of living, and had twice gone through the process of establishing a new home, new friends, and new jobs. But she had also gained a wealth of knowledge about how to minister to people in a church. She had learned more about theology than she ever imagined existed. Her faith had grown ever deeper. More than ever before, she was ready to serve. She put herself forward for potential associate pastor positions.

And then—nothing.

No positions opened up. No calls came. At first Jill was not worried. Waiting a month or two or three is not so unusual. But then six months passed. Then a year. What was wrong? She tried to keep up her hope and trust in God, but her frustration grew. She said, "The rush and excitement that comes from getting ready and then *nothing* was unbearable. I had sacrificed, worked hard, done all I believed God asked of me, so why the dead end? Did I miss something in the interpretation of the call? Was God angry with me for some sin I didn't confess?"

Jill waited a second year.

Then she waited a third year.

Her life had been sidetracked onto a painful detour. She had no explanations, only questions: Why is this happening? How long will it last?

Moses Takes a 40-year Detour on the Road to Becoming a Leader

Detours are nothing new. The Bible is full of them. Consider the life of Moses. If the Promised Land was Moses' ultimate destination, then it's hard not to see his life as a series of long and no doubt baffling detours.

I'm not referring only to his most famous detour, those 40 years he spent wandering the desert with the Israelites on their way to Canaan. What about before that? After being rescued as an infant by Pharaoh's daughter, Moses grows up in Pharaoh's household. When he's 40 years old, however, he takes a huge step toward being the liberator of the Hebrews. In Exod. 2 he decides to identify himself not with his privileged Egyptian upbringing but rather with his fellow Hebrews, who are slaves: "It happened at that time that Moses grew and went out to his brothers and saw their burdens" (Exod. 2:11, Alter). When he sees an Egyptian striking a Hebrew man, Moses takes the audacious step of siding with the slave and killing the Egyptian.

Does this act launch Moses' career as a freedom fighter? Does it trigger the other slaves to rise up in support of Moses and throw off the bondage of slavery? Do they shout, "Hooray! Go, Moses! Let the revolution begin!"?

No.

In fact, Moses does everything possible to conceal his deed. He doesn't even strike until he turns "this way and that" and sees that "there was no man about" (Exod. 2:12, Alter). Then he hides the body in the sand.

No one steps up to support him. The next day after he goes out again and tries to break up a brawl between two slaves, one of the "brother" Hebrews sarcastically dismisses him with the question "Who set you as a man prince and judge over us?" (Exod. 2:14, Alter). Talk about a put-down! This story is starting to sound decidedly unheroic.

But it gets worse. Pharaoh learns about the slaying of the Egyptian and decides to kill Moses. Not only has Moses lost hope of leading the Hebrews, he can't even retreat back into the luxury of Pharaoh's court. He has to flee, never to return. Where does he go? To some pampered life in exile? No. To a dusty desert land called Midian. The picture is sad: "and Moses fled from Pharaoh's presence and dwelled in the land of Midian, and he sat down by the well" (Exod. 2:15, Alter).

What must Moses have thought about the direction of his life at this moment? Could he have envisioned that he was on the way to becoming one of the most important figures in biblical history?

Certainly not. He was on the run, a wanted criminal. Who could blame him if he felt abandoned by God?

Moses' life had seemingly taken a dangerous and possibly irreversible detour. We know that this period in Midian is only temporary, but Moses doesn't know that. A digression is far more bearable if the person knows it's a temporary delay. For all Moses knows, he's stuck in Midian forever. This detour stretched on for *40 years*. How must Moses have felt two years, three years, five years, or 27 years into this diversion? What would we do in his place? Would we give up on God? Assume He was finished with us?

A "Spoiled Brat" Takes a Detour

Of all the people in the Bible who faced being sidetracked, few had as many detours as Joseph, and few provided a better example of how to handle them. Like the bold young Moses, who killed the Egyptian overseer, Joseph also started out brash, neglecting to weigh the full consequences of his words and actions. Old Testament scholar Robert Alter refers to the young Joseph as a "spoiled brat."[1] The first story we're told about Joseph as a teenager is that he brought his father "a bad report" about his brothers (Gen. 37:3). Alter writes, "The first revelation of Joseph's character suggests a spoiled younger child who is a tattletale."[2]

Joseph was their father's favorite, and his brothers hated him for it. Heedless of their feelings, Joseph told his brothers of two dreams he had. In the first, he and his brothers were binding sheaves in the field, and his sheaf rose and stood up, while their sheaves bowed toward his. In the second dream the sun, moon, and eleven stars bowed to Joseph. Both dreams indicated that he would eventually reign and rule over them (Gen. 37:5-11).

Even though Joseph fueled his brothers' resentment by rubbing these dreams in their faces, his arrogant attitude did not change the fact that the dreams actually did eventually come true. They were an accurate description of what was in store. Amazingly, this self-absorbed, narcissistic kid would become Pharaoh's right-hand man and help prevent a whole nation from perishing in a famine.

But not yet. Before he was called upon to run a nation, Joseph would have to endure a series of detours well beyond even what his vivid mind could have dreamed.

First, his brothers flung him into a pit (Gen. 37:24). Lying in that dark hole, he was stripped of his colorful tunic, deprived of food and water, and left to die. His grandiose dreams of the bowing sheaves and bowing stars must have seemed a cruel mockery.

Before long, however, he got pulled out of the pit! Great! Was it time now for the dream to come true? Not so fast. He was hauled out of the hole only to be sold into slavery and dragged away to Egypt (Gen. 37:27-29). A slave in a foreign country! That was about as far from his dream as he could get. How could he hold on to any hope that God was still at work in his life?

But his life was about to get thrown even farther off course. He did the best he could as a slave, but then his master's wife accused him of sexual assault. He was innocent! Far from assaulting her, he had actually rebuffed her sexual advances. No matter—he was a slave. Nobody believed him, and he was thrown into prison (Gen. 39:7-20). For all he knew, he would spend the rest of his life there.

Slave. Prisoner. Neither one was hinted at in his dreams! What was God up to?

Detours: Some Hints for Survival

Jill. Moses. Joseph. Three followers of God stuck in long detours beyond their control.

What do we do during our own detours? My own temptation is to focus too exclusively on the circumstances I'm in and to fear that perhaps that's all there is or will ever be. The big picture of my life is beyond my range of sight, so it's hard to imagine how God can take a bleak present and make it fit into a story that is ultimately triumphant. I mistake the detour for a final destination.

All three people whose stories have been told in this chapter emerged from their detours even stronger than when they entered them. How? They never lost track of two important points:

1. **Detours are not a time to shut down. They're not what we expected or wanted, but God can use them to make all the difference in our journey if we make the best of them and don't give in to discouragement or cynicism.**

How did Joseph react to his detours? Did he give up on God? Get bitter? Rage against the unfairness of his circumstances and plot revenge on those who put him there?

No. Instead, he treated these times not as detours but as if they were a part of his life's plan. Even in the worst of circumstances, he made use of whatever skills and talents he was allowed to use. He tackled his unwanted assignments with the enthusiasm of a young man who had just been hired for his dream job. Furthermore, he succeeded. Genesis 39:2 says, "The LORD was with Joseph, and he was a successful man" (NKJV).

A successful man? Is this talking about later, when Pharaoh promoted him to run the country? No, it's when he was a *slave* in Potiphar's house.

> And his master saw that the Lord was with him, and all that he did the Lord made succeed in his hand, and Joseph found favor in his eyes and ministered to him, and he put him in charge of the house, and all that he had placed in his hands. And it happened from the time he put him in charge of his house and of all he had, that the Lord had blessed the Egyptian's house for Joseph's sake and the Lord's blessing was on all that he had in house and field (Gen. 39:2-5, Alter).

What about when Joseph was in prison? Surely his life would be characterized by resentment and exasperation for being jailed for a crime he did not commit in a country where he did not belong. Not Joseph. Scripture says,

> And he was there in the prison-house, and God was with Joseph and extended kindness to him, and granted him favor in the eyes of the prison-house warden. And the prison-house warden placed in Joseph's hands all the prisoners who were in the prison-house. . . and whatever he did, the Lord made succeed" (Gen. 39:21-23, Alter).

This is not to say that Joseph was *happy* to be a slave or a prisoner or that he understood how those detours fit into God's purposes. He didn't want to prolong these detours one minute longer than was necessary. But while he was in these places, he didn't allow himself to be overtaken by resignation or self-pity. He *behaved* as if he were fulfilling God's plan.

Joseph was pushed into his painful circumstances by others—his brothers, Potiphar's wife, the forgetful cupbearer—but he trusted in God to make it right. Later, in a moving scene of reconciliation with his brothers, Joseph uttered some of my favorite words in Scripture: "While you meant evil toward me, God meant it for good, so as to bring about at this very time keeping many people alive" (Gen. 50: 20, Alter).

2. Detours are temporary. To us, God's timing and methods often look strange and meandering, but He'll get us to our destination if we trust Him to do things His way.

After finishing seminary, Jill waited three long years for a church position to open up. Finally a church called her to be an associate pastor, a position in which she served in a thriving ministry for five years. She said that a turning point in that long period of waiting happened one Sunday when she heard a message on Jesus' raising Lazarus from the dead. "In that sermon the pastor expounded on the idea that sometimes our hopes and dreams appear to be dead, that Christ lollygagged and came too late to rescue us, that the death of our hopes had even rotted in the grave and began to stink."

The way everyone *expected* Jesus to help Lazarus—to heal him *before* he died—had passed, but Jesus surprised everyone by using His own unusual timing and method to solve this seemingly unsolvable problem. He waited until Lazarus died and then resurrected him. The pastor urged his listeners to "roll away the stone from the entrance to your hearts and let Christ perform a miracle."

She said, "I realized I had put my life on hold until God gave in to my pleas. God did not work through me until I was willing to let go of my agenda, my personal desires, and my need for answers. I had to be willing to let God perform a miracle His way. It was about three months later that I received my first assignment in ministry."

Are you stuck in a detour right now? Consider this: What if this detour is not a dead end but is instead a crucial part of the journey you and God are making? What if God is working in your life in ways you can't see at the moment? These issues are part of another important principle of waiting, which we'll consider in the next chapter.

Questions for Reflection

1. Think of a period of your life you considered at the time to be a detour but that you now understand was a necessary part of your journey with God. How did that detour change you in ways you now see as beneficial?

2. Put yourself in Joseph's shoes. God gives you a dream for a bright future, but then you get tossed into a pit, sold into slavery, and unfairly imprisoned. How would you hold onto your hope and trust in God? Have you faced detours like this in your own life? How did you work through them?

3. In Gen. 50:20 Joseph says, "While you meant evil toward me, God meant it for good, so as to bring about at this very time keeping many people alive" (Alter). Can you think of other examples in which God turned evil intentions into good results?

4. Imagine that your Christian friend Mary comes to you for advice during a time when she feels stuck in one of life's long detours. Your friend feels tempted to simply shut down spiritually and do nothing until her life gets back on the path she thought she was following. What lessons from the lives of Joseph or others in this chapter might help your friend keep spiritually alive during this period?

Two

PRINCIPLE 2

Assume that God is at work— even when you don't understand what He's doing.

FRIENDS, when life gets really difficult, don't jump to the conclusion that God isn't on the job. Instead, be glad that you are in the very thick of what Christ experienced. This is a spiritual refining process, with glory just around the corner. . . .

So if you find life difficult because you're doing what God said, take it in stride. Trust him. He knows what he's doing, and he'll keep on doing it (1 Pet. 4:12-13, 19, TM).

Picture an afternoon in dusty Midian as Moses tends his flocks. It's been a hard day. His back hurts. He's hungry. He's tired of the smell of sheep. He daydreams of regal luxury in Egypt, which he fled 27 years ago. Or was it 28? He's lost track of time. Nothing has turned out right. He could have been a leader! If God had not abandoned him to these stinky animals, he could have served the Lord with passion and commitment. Where is God? Why has He chosen not to do anything more in his life?

What Moses could not have known in that moment was that the most eventful days of his life were still ahead. He faced many more years of watching over his flocks, but then he would hear God's voice in the burning bush and confront Pharaoh as leader of the Hebrews amid plagues of frogs and insects and thunder and hail. He would part a sea, he would receive the Ten Commandments from God, and he would lead his people on a dramatic 40-year trek to the Promised Land.

But this story raises questions in my mind. If God had seen fit, He could have arranged it so that Moses could have fulfilled his purpose without all the decades of waiting. If we jump ahead in the story for a moment, we see that what finally compels Pharaoh to let the Hebrew slaves go is God's power in the form of all those devastating plagues. If God had appeared before Moses in the burning bush earlier, at around the time Moses killed the Egyptian overseer, that would have saved Moses from those long years as a shepherd in Midian, and it would have spared the Israelites more miserable decades of enslavement. Why didn't He?

Similarly, if we look again at Joseph's life, God could have arranged circumstances so that Joseph's early dreams of the bowing sheaves and the bowing stars could have come true without the pain and waiting. God gave Joseph the dream and let him know the basic outline of the final outcome—so why not make it happen right away?

Many of us ask the same kinds of questions about our own lives: *If God has a spouse for me, why doesn't He bring that person into my life right now? If God has called me to work in this profession, then why can't I find a job? If God wants us to be parents, then why do we struggle with infertility?*

Was Moses' time in Midian wasted? Or was God doing some crucial work in Moses' life during those long years in the desert? Scripture gives only a few details, but consider this: When Moses first shows up in Midian and sits down by that well, the women who see him there describe him as "an Egyptian" (Exod. 2:19). He will eventually be known as the man who *liberated* the Hebrews from Egypt, but at this point he has not fully taken on a Hebrew identity. Martin Buber comments, "The narrator stresses the fact that Moses had not already become part and parcel of his brethren before his flight but retained Egyptian costume and manners. . . . He had not passed through the degrading forms of life involved in the slave status, like other Hebrews."[1]

Whether he intended to or not, Moses conveyed the identity of an Egyptian who had grown up in privileged circumstances. How could he lead the Hebrews if he was not one of them? His time in Midian would take care of that. As Buber explains,

> Moses came back to his forefathers by way of his flight. For the customs and order of life in the tribe which he entered closely resembled in their character the customs and order of life of the "fathers" of Israel. A man of the enslaved nation, but the only one not enslaved together with them, had returned to the free and keen air of his forebears.[2]

Before Midian, was the hot-headed man who killed the Egyptian overseer and hid his body in the sand *mature* enough to stand up to a heart-hardened Pharaoh and then lead a nation of suddenly liberated slaves? Moses would not have the luxury of presiding over a prosperous nation in peaceful times, but instead he would guide a complaining, disobedient nation on a 40-year journey through a dangerous desert. Was he *ready* for that before Midian?

Maybe God used Moses' time in Midian to make him truly one of his people, as Buber suggests, and to mature him and to build qualities of leadership and stability in him.

Moses got married and raised a family there. He worked hard and earned a living. God may not have spoken to him audibly from a bush during those years, and God may not give many hints about his future while he is there, but He was doing plenty inside him during those crucial years. As John J. Davis says, "The long years in the desert were not wasted years but times of further maturity and reflection in the things of God (cf. Acts 7:29 ff.). Moses needed the discipline of physical toil and the lessons this kind of occupation conveys."[3]

Joseph: From Tattletale to Ruler

What about Joseph? Could he accuse God of not doing anything significant in him during his years of waiting? Certainly not. Contrast the 17-year-old Joseph who tattles on his brothers and speaks to them in self-aggrandizing tones with the wise, mature Joseph in his 30s who ably leads a nation through crisis and extends mercy and forgiveness to his family.

The difference between the first portrait of Joseph and the later one could not be greater. Joseph did not always see or understand what God was doing. He wanted out of the pit, wanted to be freed from slavery, wanted to be released from prison. But God was doing life-changing work on him during that time.

How About Us? Is God Absent, or Is He Working?

What about us? Will we submit to God's timing and let Him complete His work in us? It's at this point of a long wait that I protest, *But I'm ready, and I've been ready for a long time. I'm tired of waiting!*

Am I really the best judge of my own readiness? Moses

thought he was ready when he killed the Egyptian. Joseph thought he was ready when he dreamed his grandiose dreams. He didn't realize he was immature. Most immature people don't. They can understand it only after the fact, if ever. If God is doing a work inside me, I may not be able to see or understand what it is until He has already completed it. Will I stick with Him in the meantime?

God was changing Moses and Joseph from the inside out, but His actions were not focused solely on them as individuals. His timing also was connected to forces and people far beyond them—the actions of Pharaohs, the history of nations, the forces of nature. Joseph in prison and Moses in the desert would have been only dimly aware of these circumstances, if they understood them at all. God would call them when the circumstances were right, but would they still be following Him and waiting on Him by then?

Popping the Question—12 Years Later

Chris and Dana, a married couple in their 40s, live in southern California with their two daughters. It's hard to imagine two people better suited to each other. Dana is a part-time consultant with her own business, and Chris is a college professor. They're committed Christians. They've purposely carved out plenty of time for family and have been involved in missions and church ministries their whole adult lives.

Their lives appear to have effortlessly fallen into place. Looking at them now, you would guess that they probably met in their early 20s, that they got engaged a few months later, and that it was smooth sailing from then on.

It wasn't that easy. They did meet when Chris was 22 and Dana was 18 and a freshman in college. At that first meeting they had no idea they were starting a friendship that would lead to marriage. And they could never have dreamed that the marriage would be 12 years in the making.

The story of those 12 years is a vivid example of how God may be at work in our lives changing us and preparing our future even when we have no idea of where He's taking us.

Dana immediately had a crush on Chris, and she thought he was flirting with her, but he later said he wasn't. In any case, she said, "If he had shown an interest, I would have dated him." It was not to be. He was a graduate student in San Diego, she was in college a couple thousand miles away, and the distance kept any romantic sparks from fanning into a larger flame. They stayed loosely connected through mutual friends and would see each other a couple of times a year.

That could have been the end of the story, but circumstances brought them together again when both of them were living in San Diego after Dana graduated from college. She started her career as a banker and roomed with some women Chris also knew, including one he had dated. Eventually Dana ended up going to the same church Chris attended, but by then both of them were dating other people.

This might have been another good stopping point, but a few years into their time in San Diego, Chris turned up his romantic interest in Dana, sending her roses and asking her out. Once again, the timing wasn't right. Dana was dating someone else and turned Chris down. Her career was moving forward, and she was working on an master's degree in business administration. She bought her own condominium, traveled, and enjoyed being single.

Chris's life took a new direction too. He moved to the Los Angeles area to begin his teaching career. This move made any prospects for a relationship with Dana look less likely than ever. In the meantime, Dana became involved with a man, but she soon recognized dangers in the relationship and in his mental health and backed away.

Then she dated another man, but that relationship ended quickly. Dana began to take a hard look at what she wanted

in life. She had enjoyed being single, but she knew she wanted to get married and have children. She talked to a coun-
selor about what she was looking for. The traits that emerged
sounded suspiciously like those of Chris!

They were still in friendly contact, though he lived a few
hours away. By then his life had changed as well. In San
Diego he had worked for a missions organization and lived a
frugal, graduate-student kind of lifestyle, living in small rooms
or apartments. Now he lived in a condominium more suited
for, well, a married couple! And for once in the 11 years they
had known each other, he and Dana were both free of other
relationships. They got together, and this time the romantic
feelings were free to flow in both directions with no barriers.
A year later they were married.

Were those 12 years wasted? Since they were eventually
going to get together anyway, wouldn't it have been better to
get married in their early 20s instead of going through all
those years of back-and-forth and near-misses?

Dana told me, "If we had gotten married in our 20s, it
would have been a disaster. We were not meant for each other in our 20s."

Twelve years is a long time for a relationship to come together, but God was working changes inside Dana, inside
Chris, and in the circumstances of their lives. The result was
a successful marriage. There were times when Dana had
doubts about where God was taking her. "I wore the brides-
maid dress many times," she said, "and wondered if marriage
would ever happen for me." But she decided the best thing to
do was to live her life to the fullest right now. Neither she nor
Chris could have planned or predicted the outcome of their
first 12 years of knowing each other. If they had forced their
own timing on the relationship, it no doubt would have
failed. Instead, they relied on God to lead them into marriage
when the time was right.

Like Chris and Dana, most of us have only the faintest understanding of the circumstances that surround God's timing. Looking back, we may see how much sense His timing makes, but will we give up on Him before we get that far?

It's easy to become resigned to the false idea that God is no longer working in our lives. We see ourselves no longer as committed followers waiting on Him to work out His perfect timing in our lives but rather as abandoned children who once knew His favor but now play no part in His story. When that happens, the danger is that once His call finally comes, we will have redefined ourselves and moved so far away from Him that we won't be able to answer. This question of our identity is at the heart of the next principle of waiting, which we'll explore in the next chapter.

Questions for Reflection

1. During the long years in the Midian desert, Moses let God do His work in him. Moses made the best of those years—obeying God, marrying, raising a family, doing the work that was placed before him. What if he had not reacted that way to this "detour" in his life? Construct an alternate history for Moses in which he lets disappointment, bitterness, or cynicism have control in his life because of his circumstances. What would have happened to him? What does that tell us about what to do in our own lives when it *appears* that God is doing nothing?

2. Besides Moses and Joseph, what other biblical figures endured long periods in which God seemed to be doing nothing but was actually fulfilling His purposes? Put yourself in their shoes and imagine how you might have felt during those long periods of waiting on God. What about Abraham? David? Jeremiah? Zechariah and Elizabeth? Others?

3. When Joseph was in prison and when Moses was out in the desert tending the flocks, do you think most of the

people around them were encouraging about their future and what God was doing in their lives? Or do you think many of them would have considered these men washed up or at a dead end? What do you think people said to them? What does that tell us about our response to the naysayers in our own lives?

Three

PRINCIPLE 3

Remember your
identity in God
during the
long days of
waiting.

BARBARA EHRENREICH is a wealthy, famous, well-educated journalist and author. In order to do research for her book *Nickel and Dimed: On (Not) Getting By in America*, she set aside the perks of her wealth and status, including her home, bank account, and comfortable lifestyle, and set out to see if she could make a living as a minimum-wage worker. She tried this experiment in three different cities, working as a waitress, a maid, and a Wal-Mart associate. She held on to certain aspects of her real identity, such as her name, clothes, and hairstyle, but she did not tell her coworkers who she really was.

Her main objective was to test the economics of living on the minimum wage, but she also wondered if she could be believable as a waitress or a maid, or would her real identity seep through? She wrote,

Several times since completing this project I have been asked by acquaintances whether the people I worked with couldn't, uh, *tell*—the supposition being that an educated person is ineradicably different, and in a superior direction, from your workaday drones. I wish I could say that some supervisor or coworker told me even once that I was special in some enviable way—more intelligent, for example, or clearly better educated than most. But this never happened, I suspect because the only thing that really made me "special" was my inexperience.[1]

Barbara Ehrenreich discovered that identity is adaptable. People accept her as a famous author when she's presented as one, but they're equally willing to accept her as a maid or waitress when she appears in those roles.

What is your identity? Do you immediately think of your profession—*I am a teacher, I am an artist, I am an electrician?* Or do you think of your relationship to others—*I am a mother, I am a husband, I am a son?* Or do you think of your identity in the church—*I am a Christian, I am a Catholic, I am a Nazarene?*

Throughout the Christian life, God often wants to move us from one identity to another. If you don't believe that, take a quick glance at the Bible. Abram becomes Abraham. Saul becomes Paul. A shepherd boy named David becomes a giant-killer and king. Jeremiah becomes a prophet. Joseph becomes a ruler. On and on the list could go. The question we must answer is *How willing am I to allow God to redefine me?*

Many of us get stuck in one identity and refuse to see ourselves in any other way. This was true with biblical figures, who often resisted—at least at first—God's new identity for them, and it's true for us today. Some of us get stuck in identities like this:

I am the guy who can't hold a job.

I am the songwriter whose songs no one sings.

I am the woman God usually ignores on His way to doing big things in other people's lives.

I am the person who has failed at every major endeavor I ever tried.

Negative identities are not the only ones that can put a stranglehold on us. We might also get stuck in these:

I am good at this profession, and I will never consider becoming anything else.

I could become that if I weren't so shy [short, unworthy, poor]—but God would never answer my prayers to move into that identity.

No matter how long you've been stuck in one identity, what if God swooped in and gave you a new vision of yourself? Would you be willing to take the risk of moving into it?

Can Moses the Shepherd Redefine Himself?

When we last saw Moses, he was working long hours guiding sheep around the desert. Did he enjoy this work? We don't know for sure. How did it compare to his days of luxury and learning and entertainment as a prince of Egypt? John J. Davis writes, "Compared to all the privileges enjoyed in the royal court, life in the desert must have been lonely and, at times, very depressing."[2] Did Moses believe that "shepherd" was his permanent identity, or did he expect God to do something else in his life?

One day as Moses is minding his own business, spending time with his sheep in one of the more obscure parts of the wilderness, he's forced to make the most important decision of his life, one that will forever alter his identity. God speaks to him from a burning bush. He tells Moses that He has seen the oppression of His people in Egypt and has chosen Moses to be the one to go to Pharaoh and demand that the Israelites be freed so they can go to the land flowing with milk and honey.

Moses' first response to God in the burning bush shows how remote God's plan must have seemed to him during those long years in the Midian desert. Remember that many years before, right after he had killed the Egyptian, the Hebrew slave had said derisively to Moses, "Who set you as a man and judge over us?" (Exod. 2:4, Alter). Now, with God speaking audibly to him and actually calling him to lead the Hebrews, Moses' response sounds like an ironic echo of that Hebrew slave. He says, "Who am I that I should go to Pharaoh and that I should bring out the Israelites from Egypt?" (Exod. 3:11, Alter).

Who am I?

We want to shout out, *You're Moses, for heaven's sake! Jump at this chance! Let the adventure begin!*

But Moses doesn't yet see himself in the heroic role. He has just spent decades tending flocks and raising his family. The circumstances that have surrounded him for years have not indicated that God is going to do much with him. Judging by events alone, Moses easily could conclude that his days of adventure are long behind him.

So when God calls him to do something that will disrupt his life forever (and in purely human terms might even appear suicidal), Moses does not eagerly embrace the opportunity. He has been waiting on God so long that he seems to have settled into a comfortable routine and no longer has the passion for action he had when he intervened with the abusive Egyptian years earlier.

This reluctance to move into a new identity is so common that Alter and other biblical scholars have identified it as a recurring scene among Old Testament prophets. When God calls Jeremiah, for example, he answers, "Ah, Lord God! Behold, I cannot speak, for I am a youth" (Jer. 1:6, NKJV). Isaiah at the time of his call declares, "Woe is me, for I am undone! Because I am a man of unclean lips, And I dwell in the midst of a people of unclean lips; For my eyes have seen the King, the LORD of hosts" (Isa. 6:5, NKJV). More than any of these prophets, Alter argues, "Moses has particular cause to feel unworthy. Having been reared as an Egyptian prince, he has become an outlaw, an exile, and a simple shepherd. His one intervention, moreover, with his Hebrew brothers elicited only a resentful denunciation of him as a murderer."[3]

Outlaw. Exile. Shepherd. Murderer. Has Moses so inhabited one or more of these identities that it causes him to question whether God has really called the right person? Part of the reluctance of Moses, Isaiah, and Jeremiah can be attributed to a sensible humility. After all, on their own, none of these men is worthy of or even capable of the great tasks to which he is called. But the reluctance also highlights a common danger all of us are prone to, which is that *a long wait can gradually eat away at our identity. We assume that because we have been stuck in this role so long, this must be who we truly are. We latch onto this assumption so automatically that we block out even the possibility for new opportunities.*

Yet we know from Scripture and from experience that surprise and change are hallmarks of the way God works:

Did Noah expect to build an ark?

Did Jonah expect to be swallowed by a fish?

Did David expect to be a king?

Did Paul expect to be an apostle?

Did Jesus' disciples expect to be pulled from their roles as fishermen or tax collectors to serve in the inner circle of the Son of God?

Rejecting the False Limitation: "That's Just Not Me"

For a number of years I served as faculty advisor to the student newspaper staff at my university. One of my most important duties was to recruit new student editors to replace the ones who graduated or left the paper. Most of them came from my Introduction to Journalism course. All semester I watched for students with the qualities of an editor—journalistic skills, discipline, consistency in meeting deadlines, and other traits.

When I found someone like that, I would invite the student to apply for one of the editor positions for the following school year. The most common response was "I have no experience. I don't know how to do layout and design on the computer. I've never . . ."

I would respond, "But you have the qualities I'm looking for. I'm confident you'll succeed. We'll train you on the details, but I believe you have the character and ability to do this job."

In other words, I tried to convince the student to try a new identity, to *see* himself or herself as an editor, and to trust that I had made these choices so many times before that I knew something about how to predict who had what it took to make it. It was a thrill to see students move from "I'm unqualified" to "I'm an editor." They *became* editors and then wondered why they ever doubted that they could.

Moses' reluctance to take on the role that God has for him is understandable. In human terms, he was *not* qualified for the position. Neither was David qualified to slay Goliath or become king. Neither was Paul qualified to become an apostle of Christ. Neither were Jesus' disciples qualified to accompany the Son of God throughout His earthly ministry. All these people had to radically redefine their identities once God showed up and said, in essence, *You've seen yourself in a certain way for a long time, but now I want to do something completely new in your life. Will you obey Me? Will you stake everything on this new vision and trust Me for the abilities, the resources, the outcome?*

He may say the same thing to us. Will we be ready to move when He does, or have we frozen our identity in place?

Questions for Reflection

1. Think of a time when the Lord moved you into a new identity. What was your initial reaction? Fear? Resistance? Excitement? How did you work through it?

2. Identify the factors that cause us to get stuck in negative identities ("I'm the person who always starts things but never finishes them"). What can we do to defeat these self-definitions and allow ourselves to move into the roles God has opened for us?

3. Have you known people who have surprised you by their change of identity? Perhaps a friend from high school who didn't seem to have much potential but who ended up achieving something big. What does your friend's experience show you about the possibilities of moving from one identity to another?

4. Study biblical figures who resisted God's new vision for them, such as Moses, Jeremiah, and Isaiah. What was the basis of their resistance? What was God's response? What can that tell us about God's calling in our lives?

Four

PRINCIPLE 4

Trust God—even though you're likely to feel His way is not the best way.

RAISING OBJECTIONS to God's methods and timing is a common activity in Scripture. Abraham does it. Job does it. Jonah does it. Moses does it. Jeremiah does it. David does it. Just as God often seems slow to act, it's also true that His methods of accomplishing His purposes often contradict the more straightforward approaches we would use if we were in charge.

Here's the challenge we face as Christians: If we can finally get to the place in which we trust His *timing*, will we also reach the point in which we trust His *methods*, even if they mean more hassle, more struggle, more interruptions, more seemingly dead ends, more risk, more imagination?

Lord, Maybe This Is Not Such a Great Idea

Moses is not so sure God has adequately thought through what He presents to him from the burning bush. For this to work, not only will Moses have to convince Pharaoh to go along with this scheme, but he'll also have to convince the Israelites that God appeared to him and told him to represent them. He says to God, "But, look, they will not believe me nor will they heed my voice, for they will say, 'The Lord did not appear to you'" (Exod. 4:1, Alter).

Do you see his point? It's one thing to follow a private calling from the Lord, but when it involves putting yourself on the line and asking others to share this vision, you open yourself up to mockery and derision. Moses has already faced this *who-do-you-think-you-are?* attitude from his fellow Hebrews in the aftermath of the killing of the Egyptian, and he's not eager to go through that again.

God answers this objection by giving Moses the signs that he can perform with the staff turning into a snake and his hand turning leprous and returning to normal again. Is that enough to reassure Moses? Not really. He raises another objection: "Please, my Lord, no man of words am I, not at any time in the past nor now since You have spoken to Your servant, for I am heavy-mouthed and heavy-tongued" (Exod. 4:10-11, Alter). He doesn't feel adequate for this mission. Even though all his years of waiting up to this point have been imposed by God, now it's Moses who wants to delay. *Send someone else* is his suggestion. It's hard to blame him. Even if Moses were a gifted orator, God's plan appears fraught with unanswered questions. What are the *details* of how Pharaoh's hand will be forced? If God wants to set the Israelites free, why do it this way? Why can't He simply sweep Pharaoh aside first and then send Moses in?

I Don't Mean to Complain, But . . .

Like Moses, I don't want to disobey God, but I also would like some assurances that if I step out in faith, I won't be stuck out there on my own. I would like to see the full plan so that I could consider it and perhaps suggest a few changes. Unfortunately, I have to admit that this is an elaborate way of saying that I don't want to have to rely solely on trusting Him.

God never does provide Moses with many details about freeing the Israelites from Pharaoh. Moses knows the broad outline, but that plan (*Walk up to Pharaoh and simply demand that he set his slaves free*) appears fraught with danger and is not reassuring. God answers Moses' objections with concrete reassurances, but only up to a point. He provides him with the signs to perform and gives him Aaron as a spokesman, but beyond that, Moses will have to decide either to disobey or else stake his very life on what God has asked him to do and believe that somehow He'll make it work.

Remember the first question Moses asks God when the Lord speaks to him from the burning bush: "Who am I that I should go to Pharaoh and that I should bring out the Israelites from Egypt?" God's answer to that is, "For I will be with you" (Exod. 3:12, Alter). That doesn't exactly answer the question, does it? Moses is worried about his own adequacy and his own identity, but God switches the subject to himself.

And yet if Almighty God is with Moses, what else does he need? Moses could be the weakest or strongest person on earth, and that would be irrelevant because it would still be God's infinitely greater power that he would rely on.

One of the reasons God's methods seem strange to us is that we're used to counting on what we see as *our own* strengths and attributes to get us through life. When God changes the subject and says, *Stop looking at whether or not you can do this, and instead think about whether I can do it*, then what He asks us to do—or what He asked Moses to do—makes more sense.

Paul faced this same dilemma of learning to stop depending on his own strength and learning to depend on God's. Paul wrote that he suffered from an unspecified "thorn in my flesh, a messenger of Satan, to torment me" (2 Cor. 12:7). Why would God make Paul endure that when Paul was doing all he could to serve God? Couldn't he do a better job if it were removed? He wrote, "Three times I appealed to the Lord about this, that it would leave me, but he said to me, 'My grace is sufficient for you, for power is made perfect in weakness.' So I will boast all the more gladly of my weaknesses, so that the power of Christ may dwell in me. Therefore I am content with weaknesses, insults, hardships, persecutions, and calamities for the sake of Christ; for whenever I am weak, then I am strong" (2 Cor. 12:8-10, NIB).

"My grace is sufficient for you." That's similar to what the Lord told Moses: "For I will be with you." For many of us, it's a frustrating answer. We come to God not to hear, "Your power is made perfect in weakness." We would really rather hear, "You can have all the power you want! I'll make you strong and impressive and wipe away all the distractions from your life—sickness, money problems, insults, critics, you name it—and you'll astound everyone with your magnificence." Instead, God lets some of those troubles remain, but He tells us not to worry because His grace, not our greatness, will be sufficient. Power is made perfect in weakness. Obviously, it's not the method we might have chosen, but how will we respond to it?

One of my weaknesses is that in arguments I can never think of clever comebacks until hours or days after the dispute. Days later, I'll think, *Oh, that would have been a perfect remark to shoot back at them! That would have shown them.* Instead, if I'm under assault in a verbal dispute, I tend to freeze up, my brain unable to form the zingers that would put my opponent in his or her place. I've envied those who spar with verbal lightning. I'm weak in that area, and yet how many times has that weakness saved me from saying words that would win the argument but cause permanent damage in a relationship? Should I ask God to remove that weakness or allow Him to use it?

Another weakness that causes great difficulties for many people is shyness. I recently read an article in *Time* magazine that told of new research that had been conducted to try to better understand and treat the problem. The most interesting part of the story to me was how it concluded:

> It would be a mistake, however, to think that therapy can eradicate all shyness—and it would be a bigger mistake even to try. Shy children may have a smaller circle of friends than more outgoing kids, but studies show they tend to do better in school and are significantly less inclined to get caught up in violence, crime, or gangs. "Shyness has a risk factor," says professor of social work J. David Hawkins of the University of Washington in Seattle. . . . "But it has a protective quality too."[1]

Weakness or strength? It depends on how it's used. The article also points out that Abraham Lincoln, Mohandas Gandhi, Nelson Mandela, and T. S. Eliot not only were shy, but also would have accomplished far less if they had not been. God can use shyness, brashness, or any other quality, and it is equally true that our "strengths," if used apart from God, can undermine us just as quickly as any "weakness."

Moses Tries Things God's Way

To Moses' credit, he finally sets aside his objections and obeys God. Despite his feelings of inadequacy, he steps out in faith and approaches the Israelites. He and Aaron tell the people all the Lord had said, and Moses performs the signs that God had given him. Astonishingly, the people actually believe him! God was right after all.

Now we might think Moses' time for waiting and delays is over. Sure, he endured that detour in Midian, and then he was a little hesitant to step into his role, but now he has God's promise and the Israelites behind him, so let's roll! Let's brush aside Pharaoh and zip on up to the Promised Land, right?

Wrong. Moses still faces some more hard lessons, and we'll consider one of them in the next chapter.

Questions for Reflection

1. God tells Moses, "I will be with you" (Exod. 3:12). He tells Paul, "My grace is sufficient for you, for my power is made perfect in weakness" (2 Cor. 12:9). Have you faced times in life when that was your only assurance to hang onto? Did you find yourself wanting a more specific answer? Is this answer enough?

2. We have seen that everyone from Moses to Isaiah to Jeremiah raised objections to God's timing and methods. How comfortable do you feel doing that? When does challenging God turn into disobedience?

3. Paul said, "So, I will boast all the more gladly of my weaknesses, so that the power of Christ may dwell in me. Therefore I am content with weaknesses, insults, hardships, persecutions, and calamities for the sake of Christ; for whenever I am weak, then I am strong" (2 Cor. 12:9-10). Content with weaknesses? Content with hardships and insults? How hard is it to think this way? Can you think of ways in your own life or in the lives of other Christians in which God used weakness in a powerful way?

4. In Exod. 3—4 God does not get very detailed with Moses on exactly what it will take to get Pharaoh to free the Israelites, or why He is choosing to do it this way, or how long the liberation and the trip to the Promised Land will take. Why do you think He withholds that information from Moses?

Five

PRINCIPLE 5

**Wait and obey—
even as things
seem to get
worse.**

IF ANYONE deserves a break, it's Moses. At this point in the story, as he prepares to approach Pharaoh, Moses is 80 years old. He is a reluctant leader. He has tried to talk God out of choosing him for this mission, but God has rejected his excuses. Moses has risked everything to obey. Now it's God's turn to move in and make this unlikely scheme work out. The hard part should be over.

Unfortunately, the worst times haven't even started. He doesn't realize it, but Moses has several more decades of waiting, uncertainty, and hassle to face. As Moses steps into his role as leader of the Hebrews, it looks as if his worst fears are coming true.

Following God's orders, Moses approaches Pharaoh and demands the Israelites be allowed to go out to the desert for a three-day celebration. Pharaoh scoffs. He refuses to go along with this outlandish demand and also responds by clamping down on the Hebrews and making their miserable lives even harder. He tells the overseers to stop giving them straw to makes bricks. They can scrabble for their own straw! And the quota of bricks is not to be reduced.

Imagine Moses' outrage and bewilderment toward God. Moses had not wanted to get involved in the first place! He had put his credibility on the line only because of the Lord's insistence and only with His reassurances. The Israelites had trusted Moses, and now they're worse off than ever. The Israelites don't let Moses off the hook. They bitterly complain, "Let the Lord look upon you and judge, for you have made us repugnant in the eyes of Pharaoh and in the eyes of his servants, putting a sword in their hand to kill us" (Exod. 5:21, Alter).

Moses' question to God is exactly what we would expect it to be: *Why?* He asks, "My Lord, why have you done harm to this people, why have you sent me? Ever since I came to Pharaoh to speak in Your name, he has done harm to this people and You surely have not rescued Your people" (Exod. 5:22-23, Alter). All those decades of waiting on God, and this is how things turn out? Working up all that courage to obey God, and this is the thanks Moses gets? He must have longed to go back home to his family, his animals, his quiet life.

Does God apologize or comfort or appease Moses? No, He answers, "Now will you see what I shall do to Pharaoh, for through a strong hand will he send them off and through a strong hand will he drive them from his land" (Exod. 6:1, Alter).

More promises.

Is Moses willing to put himself on the line once again and hope God will come through? Can the people endure it?

Moses works up the courage to go to the suffering Israelites one more time to tell them what God has said and to gain their support. Here's how Robert Alter translates their response in Exod. 6:9: "Moses spoke thus to the Israelites, but they did not heed Moses out of shortness of breath and hard bondage."

Shortness of breath.

It's not arrogance or some other corrupt attitude that causes them to disregard Moses. It's exhaustion. Alter explains why he chose "shortness of breath" as the translation for the Hebrew word *ruah*, which can also mean "breath," "wind," or "spirit": "The slaves, groaning under hard bondage—a condition made all the harder by Moses' bungled intervention—can scarcely catch their breath and so are in no mood to listen to Moses. Others render this term as 'impatience' or 'crushed spirit.'"[1]

Many of us, if we were in Moses' shoes, would quit. He tried it God's way, and things didn't work out. Enough is enough. Moses complains to God again, pointing out that neither Pharaoh nor the Israelites are paying attention to him. Does God reassure him with a timetable of upcoming events, with new powers, or with anything new at all?

No, He simply repeats His command to go back to Pharaoh. God not only promises that Pharaoh will let the people go, but He also claims that this mighty ruler will "drive them from his land" (Exod. 6:1, Alter). Even if Moses believes that God will make this unlikely outcome occur, he still has no idea how much more he or his people will have to endure in the meantime. How much more can they stand?

What Is God Doing to Me?

Moses is not the only person in Scripture who faces this dilemma of things getting worse for a time even though he's obeying God. In fact, that seems to be a common pattern. Let's go back to Joseph. God gives him those amazing dreams as a teenager, but when Joseph tells his brothers about them, where does it get him? *Thrown into the pit and sold into slavery.* When he's a slave in Potiphar's house, he lives a life of integrity and honorably refuses to sleep with the boss's wife, but where does he end up? *Tossed into prison.* He interprets the dream for the cupbearer in prison, and what's his reward? He's *forgotten* for the next two years.

Joseph makes the best of every setback, and each tough

spot ends up being a steppingstone on the path to Pharaoh's door and helping save a nation. But in the meantime, he waits and suffers.

Or look at Jeremiah. He obeys God, but the humiliation he suffers reaches absurd levels. As Eugene Peterson puts it, Jeremiah "lived through crushing storms of hostility and furies of bitter doubt. Every muscle in his body was stretched to the limit by fatigue; every thought in his mind was subjected to questioning; every feeling in his heart was put through fires of ridicule."[2]

In what ways does he suffer? After preaching a sermon, Jeremiah gets whipped and put in the stocks in a gate of the Temple (Jer. 20). Later God tells him to make a harness and yoke and harness himself up as an illustration to the kings to whom he has to speak (Jer. 27). Later he's thrown in jail (Jer. 32). For a while he's confined in a cistern, where he sinks into the mud. Finally we see him in chains, being herded off with others to exile in Babylon (Jer. 40).

Like Moses, Jeremiah both *complains* to God and *obeys* Him. Moses' protests to God are bold, but they're nothing compared to Jeremiah's outbursts: "You pushed me into this city, God, and I let you do it. You were too much for me. And now I'm a public joke. They all poke fun at me. Every time I open my mouth I'm shouting, 'Murder!' or 'Rape!' And all I get for my God-warnings are insults and contempt" (Jer. 20: 7-8, TM). Later in the chapter he writes, "Curse the day I was born! The day my mother bore me—a curse on it, I say! . . . Why, oh why, did I ever leave that womb? Life's been nothing but trouble and tears, and what's coming is more of the same" (Jer. 20:14, 18, TM).

Just as He does with Moses and Joseph, God makes it clear that His long-term plans for Jeremiah and His people are bright. In fact, one of the most famous verses in Jer. 29:11 reads, "For surely I know the plans I have for you, says the

LORD, plans for your welfare and not for harm, to give you a future with hope" (NIB). Whenever I see this encouraging verse on posters or pictures, it appears alone, out of context. But look at the verse that appears right before it: "For thus says the LORD: Only when Babylon's seventy years are completed will I visit you, and I will fulfill to you my promise and bring you back to this place" (Jer. 29:10, NIB). Do you see how that changes the meaning of verse 11? God plans to give the people a future with hope, but only after a difficult 70-year exile.

Even though obedience to God is required in order for His plans to be fulfilled in Moses, Joseph, and Jeremiah, their obedience does not guarantee quick results. They must wait through long periods of setbacks and challenges first. The same is true of many others we could look at, such as Abraham, Job, and Paul. They endure short-term frustration and pain in order to fulfill a long-term plan of God that often extends far beyond their own lifetimes.

If all these other people of faith endured times of misery as they were following God's call, should I be surprised when it happens to me? If God worked out a long-term plan for them that was *good*, then isn't it reasonable to think He'll do so for me?

Enduring Chaos as the Lord Remodels Our Lives

It's discouraging to see things get worse when we're doing all we can to obey God, but it might help to make the following comparison to a home remodeling project. If you're renovating your house, the dust and mess are acceptable because you know they're only temporary and the house will be better off once the work is done. While the process is happening, it's uncomfortable—even miserable—but you willingly put up with it in the short run.

Now imagine this: what if all that remodeling chaos descended on your house without your approval or without your prior knowledge? What if walls suddenly collapsed, furniture was moved, carpeting was ripped out, cabinets disappeared, and you had no idea why this was happening? Would you panic? Would you try to stop it? Would you protest and complain?

That's what it's often like when God is remodeling our lives or working out a long-term plan. Our lives may be in the process of a magnificent renovation that will leave us far better off than we ever dreamed, but we're in the dark about where all this is leading. All we can see is that right now everything is a mess.

Now imagine one more thing. What if in our homes we decided we had zero tolerance for the discomfort that goes along with remodeling or repairs? If the carpet wore through, we wouldn't replace it. If the furnace died, we would go cold. If pipes burst, we would go without water. Our insistence on short-term stability would cause us long-term misery.

The same is true in many other areas of life. Why would we allow a surgeon to slice into our bodies in ways that will make us endure days or weeks of recovery? We put up with the pain and inconvenience for the sake of our long-term health. Why do athletes give up hours of their lives each day to difficult and painful training? They do it for the long-term rewards of increased physical prowess.

Spiritually, God's ways and God's timing are more complex and mysterious than house remodeling, surgery, or sports practice. The results may be harder for us to envision. Following Him in spite of visible temporary setbacks tests our faith in ways no other process in life will. But what happens to the followers of God like Moses, Abraham, Joseph, and others who obey Him in the midst of dire circumstances? Consider the principle presented in the next chapter.

Questions for Reflection

1. Moses' first confrontation with Pharaoh results in punish-

ment of the Israelites. Their lives get harder because of Moses' obedience to God. What false conclusions might the people have drawn about those circumstances? That God had not really called Moses? That God didn't plan to free them? That God was not as powerful as Pharaoh? What false assumptions might we be tempted to make when we suffer in the midst of serving the Lord? How can we avoid that destructive thinking?

2. Review the stories of Joseph, Moses, and Jeremiah. At what point in these stories might you have been tempted to quit? What kept these men going? What can we learn from that?

3. This chapter mentions home remodeling, surgery, and training for athletic competition as examples of areas in life in which we voluntarily accept short-term suffering to enjoy the long-term benefits. Can you think of other areas of life in which we do this? Is it harder to accept short-term chaos and suffering in the spiritual realm of our lives than in these other areas? Are the comparisons valid?

Six

PRINCIPLE 6

Have faith that in His good time God will sweep away the obstacles.

ALMOST. Not yet.

That's the holding pattern Moses gets caught in as he prepares to make new demands of Pharaoh. How many of us have gotten caught in that same predicament? The fulfillment of God's calling in our lives, the answers to our deepest longings seem achingly close. Yet God keeps us dangling. He doesn't say yes. He doesn't say no. Either of those answers would at least provide clarity. Instead, we twist in the wind.

A long period of waiting on God to act is fraught with dangers. One of the biggest perils is that when He doesn't follow the timetable we expected or wanted, we lose faith in Him and simply walk away. Short of an extreme move like that, however, there is another danger that's more subtle but still quite sinister: *a long wait might lead us to lower our expectations of God.* We interpret "not yet" to mean "never." We begin to believe this vague disappointment with God is a permanent condition. He'll take us so far, He'll raise our hopes, but we'll always be left stranded in the end. We don't give up exactly. We don't renounce our Christian commitment and publicly turn away from God.

Instead, we believe in Him, but we don't expect much from Him. We'll continue to call ourselves His, but we don't intend to dream big anymore or put ourselves on the line for Him. There was a time when we had that kind of big faith, but maybe it was just youthful spiritual immaturity. Now we've grown up, and we know that God takes only tiny steps, and He never seems to get where He's going.

Pharaoh surrenders! Pharaoh changes his mind. Pharaoh surrenders! Pharaoh changes his mind. Pharaoh surrenders! Pharaoh changes . . .

When Moses gets stuck in an "almost, not yet" phase—one of many that he'll have to endure in his life—he's on the verge of an astounding triumph. The Israelites are about to be set free after hundreds of years of slavery. However, Moses sees no evidence of this victory yet. We've seen his first approach to Pharaoh make the lives of the Hebrews even worse, and his own life is now more miserable also. His credibility is shot.

But then the plagues begin. *Finally God means business,* Moses must think. With Pharaoh refusing to let the Hebrews go out to worship God in the wilderness, God gives Moses and Aaron the power to turn the water of the Nile into blood, killing the fish and making the water undrinkable. When that doesn't change the mind of the heart-hardened Pharaoh, God tells Moses to announce the next plague, which comes in the form of frogs covering everything from Pharaoh's bed to his kitchen to every other place where he might turn. The frogs cause such distress that Pharaoh gives in and says, "Entreat the Lord that He take away the frogs from me and my people, and I shall send off the people, that they may sacrifice to the Lord" (Exod. 8:4, Alter).

Finally success! The "almost, not yet" phase is over, and Moses can finally lead his people away, right?

Well, as with so many other aspects of Moses' life, it isn't that simple. The Lord kills off the frogs, which are heaped up into piles that make the whole land stink, but once the crisis has passed, Pharaoh changes his mind and backs out of his agreement. He does not release the Israelites, and Moses is back where he started.

This begins a pattern of (1) plagues and the attempts of Pharaoh's magicians to match them, followed by (2) Pharaoh's surrender, followed by (3) Pharaoh's backing out of his promise to let the Hebrews go. This pattern is repeated so many times that everyone involved must have found it absurd. *Almost, not yet.*

After the frogs come lice so thick that "all the dust of the land became lice in all the land of Egypt" (Exod. 7:14, Alter). Pharaoh doesn't budge. Then comes a horde of insects that attack people and houses and the land itself.

Pharaoh then gives in again—but he changes his mind once the horde is gone.

Next comes a pestilence that kills the Egyptians' horses, donkeys, camels, cattle, and sheep. No movement from Pharaoh. Then Moses throws dust in the air, and it causes a burning rash and boils to erupt all over the Egyptians' bodies. Pharaoh still doesn't listen. After that, hail unlike anything ever seen in Egypt smashes down on the nation, demolishing everything. Pharaoh says, "The LORD is in the right, and I and my people are in the wrong. Pray to the LORD, for we have had enough thunder and hail. I will let you go; you don't have to stay any longer" (Exod. 9:27-28).

Hooray! Victory!

But what happens next?

You guessed it. Pharaoh changes his mind. How long can this go on? Moses, the Egyptians, and the Israelites must wonder whether the rest of their lives will be spent witnessing this endless series of bizarre disasters.

Almost, not yet. In case you've lost count, Moses is ready to announce plague number eight. This time it's locusts. After that, Pharaoh gives in (and then changes his mind) for the fourth time.

Plague number nine is three days of total darkness. Pharaoh surrenders yet again. Then he reverses his decision. That makes five times of surrendering and five times of backing out. Why is God putting up with this? Does He not have the power to get the job done?

There are reasons why God chooses this long, frustrating method of setting His people free. As He says in the midst of these plagues, "For by now I could have sent forth My hand and I could have struck you and your people with pestilence, and you would have been wiped off the face of the earth. And yet, for this I have let you stand—so as to show you My power, and so that My name will be told through all the earth" (Exod. 9:15-16, Alter). Alter comments, "The Exodus story is conceived as an establishing of the credentials of the God of Israel for all humankind. Hence his awesome power has to be demonstrated in one plague after another, and Pharaoh's repeated resistance is a required condition of the demonstration."[1]

That's a helpful theological explanation, but it doesn't change Moses' immediate dilemma. *He doesn't know how long this phase will last.* Will he have to announce one more plague, or 50? Will this go on for a few more days, or a few more years? If God wanted to show His power this way, wouldn't three or four plagues have been enough? *Almost, not yet.*

Just When You Thought This Standoff Would Never End . . .

Finally comes the worst plague of all. When God decides to bring this sequence of events to an end, He does it in a way that's terrifying, bold, unmistakable. The final plague involves the striking down of every firstborn in the land of Egypt, "from the firstborn of Pharaoh sitting on his throne to the firstborn of the captive who was in the dungeon, and every firstborn of the beasts" (Exod. 12:29, Alter).

These horrible deaths wipe away Pharaoh's reluctance in an instant. Now he not only *allows* the Israelites to leave, but he *insists* on it, and so do his people: "And Egypt bore down on the people to send them off from the land, for they said, 'We are all dead men'" (Exod. 12:33-34, Alter). God will not be stopped. His plan will be fulfilled.

The way God chooses to bring Pharaoh to his knees must have seemed frustratingly complicated and roundabout and miserable for Moses and his people. However, there was one important truth they held onto: *The fact that God takes a long time to accomplish His purposes does not mean He lacks the power or will to move forward.*

Sounds simple, but do we really believe this in our own lives? Or when He seems to be stalling around, doing nothing, do we let ourselves sink into discouragement because we seem to be serving a deaf, detached God? What if Moses had gotten fed up with God's slowness and quit after the fifth or sixth plague? What if we give up on the verge of God's breakthrough in our lives, when He's about to sweep in and blast away a barrier that has stood in our path for years?

Another idea Moses held onto: *The destination is not the only thing that matters.* What happens during the "waiting" part of our story is really part of our calling, not just empty time leading up to it. The part of Moses' story that's devoted to the plagues takes six chapters of Exodus. As we've seen, they're put there to establish God's credentials and show His supremacy. As exasperating as it might have been for Moses to keep pronouncing all those plagues and fighting that battle of wills with Pharaoh, we now look upon this phase as a crucial part of Moses' story. He was *fulfilling* his calling, not just *waiting* to get to it.

Whenever we're in an "almost, not yet" period, we should ask ourselves what God may be accomplishing in our lives right now—apart from whatever outcome we're waiting for. How is what we're living right now a part of the fulfillment of His call for us?

When I look back on some of the "waiting" periods of my own life, I now see those phases much differently than I did at the time. One example is graduate school. At the time, living in a tiny room and barely making a living as a teaching assistant, I saw grad school as mainly a transition phase in my life. It was the dues I had to pay on my way to serving in the career to which I felt called. I often regretted that it was taking so long. It bothered me that I felt so far behind other people my age who were already working for companies and getting married and settling into neighborhoods. I believed that my real calling would start once I finished my degree and got a "real" job.

Now, however, I look back on that period with much more appreciation, sometimes even longing. Though I had little money, I enjoyed the luxury of simplicity. I could devote all my time to studying the field I loved, learning how to teach, spending time with friends, and pursuing other good activities. I didn't have the distractions of yard work, mortgage, a house to maintain. Some of my most productive times of reading and writing and thinking happened during those years. I'm still benefiting from that experience. I wouldn't want to have stayed in grad school forever, but I now see it as part of my calling, not simply a preparation for it.

Many of us make the mistake of ignoring the opportunities before us on *this* day because we've placed all our attention on waiting for what's coming next. College becomes *only* preparation for a career; our days of being single become *only* about waiting for marriage; our days before our children are born become *only* a time of wanting to start raising a family; our days of working at our jobs become *only* a time of preparing for retirement.

It makes sense to plan for the future during those periods of our lives, but it doesn't make sense to sacrifice the life God gives us now to put all our attention on the life we hope He'll give us. Perhaps one reason He keeps us in some "almost, not yet" stages so long is that He's trying to get us to *pay attention* to each season of our lives before He moves us to the next one.

If I had it to do over again, I would have lived many seasons of my life with a greater sense of alertness and gratitude and less restlessness or just wanting to "get it over with." Gratitude is an important principle we'll examine in the next chapter.

Questions for Reflection

1. This chapter describes a time in life when the fulfillment of God's calling in our lives, the answers to our deepest longings, seem achingly close, and yet God keeps us dangling. He doesn't say yes. He doesn't say no. Either of those answers would at least provide clarity. Instead, we twist in the wind. Can you think of a time like that which you've endured? How long did it last? How was it resolved? What would you say to other Christians who are facing a similar struggle?

2. What happens during the "waiting" part of our story is really part of our calling, not just empty time leading up to it. This statement is made in the context of Moses's waiting for his people to be set free while one plague after another is visited upon Pharaoh. Can you think of other biblical stories in which the "waiting" part turns out to be just as important for that person as the destination? What about Abraham, for instance? Or David?

Seven

PRINCIPLE 7

Remind yourself of what the Lord did for you in the past.

AS A TEENAGER, I listened to loud music and spent many hours wearing headphones and dancing around my bedroom to my favorite tunes. Those hours were often a time for daydreaming. I remember one particular spot by the stereo where I stood, looked out the window, and thought, *Even though I've lived most of my life in this house and this place seems such a permanent part of me, I know that I won't always live in this room. Before long, life will take me in one of thousands of directions and places. Where will I end up? What will I do?*

At times my fantasies produced images of fame, power, and wealth. At other times, my imagination toyed with the idea of *what if nothing ever works out for me? What if no one ever wants to hire me, and my life spirals constantly downward in shame and humiliation?*

I believed God would be with me throughout my life, but He gave me only the vaguest idea of where life would take me. I put my faith in Him and moved forward.

Now, a few decades later, I look back and realize that I've

traveled a journey I never could have predicted back in that bedroom in Indiana. I've been to dozens of places I had never even heard of then. I went to college, got married, had children, bought a house, wrote books. As a young teenager, I found that even the possibility of owning a car would have been a thrill. If my teenage self could have glimpsed the life I've lived over the past 30 years, what would I have thought of it? I think I would have viewed it with a sense of wonder, gratitude, and expectancy.

I wonder—Why doesn't my current, older self see my life with the same sense of gratitude? More often I find myself taking for granted all those good things God has put into my life and focusing instead on the crisis of the moment, wondering why God is taking so long to help me through it. I feel stressed, pushed to my limit, envious of how much better other people have it.

What happens when I leave this harried mind-set and look at my life anew, as if I were introducing it to that teenage self wearing those headphones? What if, as I pull out each blessing and show it to that boy, I thank God for it?

Look at your own life and do this, and see how it changes your perspective. Pull out each blessing God has put into your life, and thank Him for it. You don't have to start with the biggest things. Thank Him for whatever occurs to you first. I thank Him for the meal I finished a few hours ago. I thank Him that for the past eight years I've lived in my home. I thank Him that I've been able to pay the mortgage each month. I thank Him for the warm sunshine outside my window. For good health. For my wife and children. For a computer to make my work easier. For a stack of books to read.

Don't stop with blessings. Go back ten years and think of the worst times you have endured. What were the crises when you feared God had forgotten you, when you were afraid you wouldn't pull through? Do you now see God's hand in the midst of any of the turmoil? Thank Him. Did He bring you through in ways you never would have expected, in ways that have made you stronger today, in ways that will help you trust Him more when the next crisis hits?

If you sat for an hour or two and added up all the blessings you could think of and all the hard times God helped you overcome, how many items would you have on your list? Fifty? A hundred? Several hundred? What difference would such a list make?

When I do this—and it's an exercise I now regularly practice—the first thing it does is change my attitude toward my life right now. Instead of feeling primarily like a man with a long list of difficulties to tackle, I feel *blessed*. I see the many ways God's grace is flowing in my life regardless of whatever trouble is at hand. Second, I realize that if God has spent all these years blessing me, and if He's brought me through all those other tough times, then I should certainly put my faith in Him now. I may be waiting on Him to act, but I don't have to be frantic in the waiting.

I recently read a *Time* magazine cover story titled "The Science of Happiness." One of the "happiness boosters" suggested in the article is a "gratitude journal—a diary in which subjects write down things for which they are thankful."[1] Can keeping a journal of this kind really make people happier? University of California at Riverside psychologist Sonja Lyubomirsky studied this and found that "taking the time to conscientiously count their blessings once a week significantly increased subjects' overall satisfaction with life over a period of six weeks, whereas a control group that did not keep journals had no such gain."[2] Another psychologist, Robert Emmons, of the University of California at Davis, found that gratitude exercises "improve physical health, raise energy levels, and, for patients with neuromuscular disease, relieve pain and fatigue."[3] University of Pennsylvania psychologist Martin Seligman found that practicing an exercise called "three blessings—taking time each day to write down a trio of things that went well and why," had long-lasting positive effects, making people less depressed and happier three months later and six months later.[4]

Stop All the Action—and Remember

Remembrance of what God has done is the message that God through Moses brings to the people in Exod. 13. Setting up the details of these rituals of remembrance is so important that it's allowed to interrupt the flow of the dramatic story that surrounds it. Just before this chapter, the firstborn of Egypt have been killed and the Israelites have gained their freedom after 400 years of slavery and the ten plagues. Just after this chapter, Pharaoh's army will pursue the Hebrews and be destroyed when the sea that Moses parts washes over them. But here all of that action stops as the people are commanded to *remember* what God has done—to pay attention to it and learn from it—and to do so as a regular part of their worship throughout the ages.

Remembrance and gratitude are so important that they are not simply left to chance, but they're *established* as a yearly ritual in the Passover celebration and other traditions that are still practiced today. The Passover commemoration is put in place to help the people constantly keep in mind who God is, what He has done, and what He can do now in their own lives. "Moses said to the people, 'Remember this day on which you came out of Egypt, out of the house of slavery, because the LORD brought you out from there'" (Exod. 13:3).

Biblical scholar John I. Durham explains the importance of this pause to remember what God has done:

> The related requirements of the ritual of Passover and Unleavened Bread and the dedication to Yahweh of every firstborn life in Israel function in Exodus as requirements of recollection. . . . Their purpose, then, is to call from the past to the present that story, to make the fathers' Exodus

experience the Exodus experience also of the sons and the sons' sons, down all the generations. Their parallels, in our own remembrance in and for worship, are the service of communion and the service of the dedication (or christening or baptism) of newborn children.[5]

Like the Passover celebration and other rituals, the very existence of the Book of Exodus and the books that surround it illustrates how God uses remembrance in the lives of believers. Alter calls the narrative in Exodus a kind of "national epic."[6] Notice, however, that it does not tell only of heroic deeds. The frailties, sins, complaints, and failures of the leaders and the people are vividly displayed. The people are commanded to remember all those things. Through every circumstance, good and bad, God keeps working, His story keeps flowing forward.

What happens when we fail to remember what God has done for us and concentrate only on our immediate crisis? We'll get some insight into the dangers of that kind of short-sightedness in the next chapter.

Questions for Reflection

1. Go back ten years, and try to remember the issues you were facing at that time. If you kept a journal then, go back and read what you wrote that year. What were you worried about? What difficulties were you dealing with? What were your hopes and dreams? Now trace the various ways God has worked in those situations from then to now. Did He surprise you in any way? Could you have predicted things would turn out the way they have? What does remembering these things show you about how God works?

2. As the chapter suggests, make a list of the good things God has put into your life, and thank Him for each one. Write down whatever comes to mind, from the smallest blessing to the largest. How long is your list? How does it change your perspective on what God has done and is doing in your life?

Eight

PRINCIPLE 8

Wait when it's time to wait and act when it's time to act.

GET TO THE Promised Land as quickly as possible.
Take no chances that this freedom could be snatched away.
Pharaoh is crazy. He's stubborn. His heart is hard. He has a
big army. He let us go, but he could change his mind at any
moment. Run!

Some of these thoughts must have been running through the minds of the Israelites after finally gaining their freedom from Pharaoh. Their desire to move quickly to the Promised Land is logical, and there's a quick route to Canaan, but God does not let them take it. That shouldn't surprise us, since we've seen time and time again in the lives of Joseph, Moses, and others that God rarely leads His followers along the fastest or most obvious route.

Exod. 13:17 says, "And it happened when Pharaoh sent the people off that God did not lead them by way of the land of the Philistines though it was close, for God thought, 'Lest the people regret when they see battle and go back to Egypt'" (Alter). As Alter explains, this faster route "by way of the land of the Philistines" to Canaan was "heavily fortified by the

Egyptians as the principal avenue for their varying imperial enterprises to the north, and so would have immediately confronted the fleeing slaves with the prospect of 'battle.'"[1]

God, of course, can bring them victory in any battle they face, just as He's worked out so many difficulties already, but He knows they're not ready to believe that. Instead, He sends them out into the wilderness near the Sea of Reeds. He has an ingenious plan in mind, but they don't know what it is. Camping out there in that wilderness looks like the worst idea imaginable. They're not getting where they want to go, and they're sitting ducks if Pharaoh decides to revoke their freedom and send his army to capture them. What will they do?

When You're Following God's Plan, Prepare to Be Second-Guessed

God's plan doesn't look too bright to Pharaoh either. The ruler of Egypt misses his huge slave workforce. He decides it's time to send out his army to bring them back. After all, those Hebrews are wandering around the desert, and they appear to have lost their way: "And Pharaoh had said of the Israelites, 'They are confounded in the land, The wilderness has closed round them'" (Exod. 14:3, Alter).

They are confounded in the land.

In fact, Pharaoh is wrong about this. The people are exactly where God wants them to be. They're obeying Him, and He has a strategy for what will happen next that will defeat Pharaoh once and for all.

Does the Israelites' dilemma sound familiar? During long times of waiting on the Lord, those around you often may believe that you are "confounded" even though you're simply obeying God. Because they don't yet see the evidence of God's work in you, naysayers may accuse you—to your face or behind your back—of laziness, lack of faith, lack of talent, or lack of drive. Even well-intentioned friends may urge you to take matters into your own hands, find a shortcut to your goal, or force an outcome. But if you're assured in your call and you're doing all that He's commanding you to do in the place of waiting, then you need not be afraid of the wilderness.

The Israelites don't see it that way. They're stuck out in the desert, and as if that weren't bad enough, Pharaoh's army is headed right toward them! What is their response? Do they *remember* what God has just brought them through and rely on Him to rescue them again? Do they consult with Moses to reassure themselves that this man of God has really brought them here at the Lord's command?

No. They panic. Just as Pharaoh second-guesses his own decisions, and just as he also misunderstands why Moses is leading the Israelites in a strange direction, so the Israelites second-guess their leader. They don't do so in calm, measured tones. They don't give Moses or God any credit for having performed miraculously for them in the past. When they decide to challenge Moses' leadership decisions, they turn on him in fear, despair, and sarcasm: "Was it for lack of graves in Egypt that you took us to die in the wilderness? What is this you have done to us to bring us out of Egypt? Isn't this the thing we spoke to you in Egypt, saying, 'Leave us alone, that we may serve Egypt, for it is better for us to serve Egypt than for us to die in the wilderness'?" (Exod. 14:11-13, Alter).

Despite this melodramatic, ungrateful verbal attack on Moses, there's no evidence the Israelites had ever told him they didn't want their freedom. On the contrary, they seemed eager to leave once they were sent away. But their harsh reaction of blame and second-guessing illustrates a danger all of us face during periods of waiting on God. By its nature, a time of waiting is a time of transition, a time of moving from a familiar place to an unknown place. The new, unknown destination can be frightening enough, but the wilderness in between us and that new place can be even scarier.

Even if God is taking us to a place where we've pleaded with Him to go, once we see that the road itself is filled with unexpected hazards, we might try to convince ourselves that we didn't really want to go there in the first place, and it would be better just to go back where we started! I once prayed fervently for a job to open up in another state. God answered that prayer, and I immediately accepted the position. Then I moved. It was a faraway place, where I knew no one. Friends and family were suddenly absent, and there I sat in a silent apartment by myself. The thought that kept running through my mind was *What have I done?* It was one thing to contemplate a new job from the safety of my familiar surroundings, but now I was in my own wilderness, stuck. Had I made a mistake?

After a month or two of homesickness, the new place became my home, I made friends, I threw myself into my work. That was the end of my second-guessing.

Unlike me, however, the Israelites had Pharaoh's chariots bearing down on them. How would Moses respond to their criticism? How would he get them out of this jam?

Take Your Station. The Lord Will Fight Your Battle for You.

Moses' answer to the panic and sarcasm of the people is full of wisdom that can help us all. The insecure Moses of earlier chapters is gone. In human terms, the situation facing him is dire, but he remembers other impossible situations God has brought him through and steps forward in faith. He says, "Do not be afraid. Take your station and see the Lord's deliverance that He will do for you today, for as you see the Egyptians today, you shall not see them again for all time. The Lord shall do battle for you, and you shall keep still" (Exod. 14:13-14, Alter).

Consider some of those phrases:

Do not be afraid.
Take your station.
The Lord shall do battle for you.
You shall keep still.

We know that earlier in the story of the Israelites, as in all our stories, there were times for swift *action*. One such time for the Hebrews was when Pharaoh sent them off. They had to pack up and go quickly. During that time there was no indication they felt any discontent or restlessness.

But just as there are times when the Lord calls us to move swiftly, there are other times when the Lord commands us *not* to act. We must "take our station." We must remain ready in a place that is a necessary step in our journey, even though it's not really where we want to be.

A good example we've seen is Joseph in prison. He has taken his station there. He does his duty, makes the best of the opportunities he finds there, interprets dreams when he can, but he never sees this jail as his final destination. It plays an important role in getting him to his destination, since the cupbearer he meets there eventually tells Pharaoh about him, but while he's in prison, he doesn't know why he is there, where it will lead, or how long he'll have to wait.

For the rest of us, "taking our station" may assume many different forms. We may sense a call to a certain profession or to a ministry within our church or toward some other dream. Even after we're fully prepared to fulfill that role and have shown our availability—for instance, by completing the necessary education or submitting the application or proposal or by showing our readiness by other means—we have to simply take our station and wait for the Lord to move.

"The Lord shall do battle for you. . . . You shall keep still." In one sense, "keeping still" sounds like the easiest command of all, but for some of us it's the hardest. We would much prefer something to *do*—a task to perform, a phone call to make

—any bit of concrete action that could help convince us we're moving forward. This is especially true in a situation like the one the Israelites were in, when their very lives are threatened by the army that's racing toward them. That is not the time people want to hear, "Keep still." They would feel more comfortable with "Run!" or perhaps "Grab a weapon and get ready to fight!" Letting the Lord fight their battle for them requires too much trust, which feels like passivity.

Many of us action-oriented people feel the same way. We reach the point at which we've done all we know the Lord wants, but our restlessness makes it excruciatingly difficult to wait on Him to fight for us. We worry, *What if He doesn't pull through for me? Will I kick myself for not forcing my own outcome?*

Sitting on the Couch in Obedience to God's Command

Dan is a successful Christian businessman who has traveled the world, sometimes on business and sometimes on missions trips. He has a master's degree in business administration and is an energetic, take-charge person. When he was 31 years old, his career was thrown off-stride when he lost his job with a major corporation. After several months of demoralizing unemployment, he landed a job with a business he thought was run by a Christian, but he quickly realized the company was riddled with unethical practices. He quit after only one week.

Unemployed for a second time, ineligible for unemployment benefits because of having willingly resigned from the second company, and running out of money to pay his bills, Dan prayed hard for God's direction. He had done all he knew to do to find a new job, but nothing worked out. His worry deepened, edging toward despair. He says, "I began to pray. I asked God to direct me. I told Him I would do what He wanted me to do but that He would have to show me the way. Nothing happened. My prayers seemed to rise no higher than the ceiling."

Knowing Dan was unemployed, some friends in his men's Bible study urged him to take this opportunity to pursue his interest in teaching English in China for a missions organization. However, he couldn't afford the cost of the three months of training or the living expenses involved, so that idea was out. After attending a Bible study one day, Dan confided his frustrations to a friend, complaining there was something seriously wrong in his life.

"How do you know there's something wrong?" his friend asked.

"Because I'm at the end of my rope, and God isn't saving me. I have no job, and my money is running out. I've asked God to direct me, but He isn't doing anything."

"How do you know He isn't doing anything?"

"I'll tell you how I know," said Dan, losing patience. "Because yesterday I did nothing. Nothing! I woke up, went downstairs, and sat on the couch. I feel like a bum and a failure. I've tried everything I know to try. If God was doing something, He wouldn't have let me sit there all day, waiting."

"Maybe you didn't sit there long enough," said his friend.

This sounded absurd. Dan didn't want to sit there *at all*, let alone *longer*. He went home feeling desperate. He prayed to the Lord, *I know you're real, and I know that you see me and care for me. I don't know what to do. I've pursued all my opportunities. You seem silent and distant. Please show me what to do. I will wait until you make the next move.*

For Dan, this was the scariest prayer of all. He said, "I didn't know if I'd have to wait an hour, a day, a week, or a year. But I knew I was committed to not making a move until God did something. Would an angel appear? Would someone come to the door and offer me the perfect job? Would I starve to death on the couch?"

Dan sat on his couch for one day, then another, then another. His roommates came and went. The sun rose. The sun set. It rose again. It set again. He said, "I wish I could say it was a spiritual experience, but it wasn't. At least not in the way you may be thinking. I didn't fast and pray. I didn't get on my knees and seek the face of God. I didn't spend hours singing and praising God for His goodness. No, I just waited in quietness and stillness. I felt numb."

When the breakthrough finally came, things moved quickly. One afternoon the telephone rang, and a friend who rarely called was on the line. He asked how Dan was doing. "I've been sitting on the couch for days," said Dan.

"Would you be interested in a job?" asked his friend.

Dan was interested. The work was temporary, a project that would make good use of his degree. The pay was exactly the amount Dan needed to live on and, if he chose, to complete the training for the trip to China. The project would last for three months, which was (coincidentally?) exactly the length of time before the China training program started. He took the job. He went to China.

Dan said, "I went from sitting on the couch one day to having a job and preparing for a year in China. Who could have imagined that sitting on a couch and doing nothing would produce such a flurry of activity and opportunity? Don't ask me to explain the theology of it all. I only know I learned a lesson about what it means to 'wait on God' that I've never heard preached in church."

He had learned to take his station and let God do battle for him. He learned to truly trust the Lord. "At the core of my faith was a big fear that maybe God couldn't make something out of nothing, even though I was taught that He's the author of Creation. The answer to that fearful question never became clear for me until the world I had created—and was feverishly trying to maintain—fell apart and came to a halt."

The Lord Fights the Israelites' Battle

Just as God worked out a solution for Dan that went beyond anything he could have devised, in the Exodus story He also comes through for the Israelites in the wilderness in ways *their own efforts could never have come close to matching.* As the Egyptian army draws near, Moses stretches out his hand over the sea, and the Lord causes the water to split apart to form a dry area for the Hebrews to cross. The Egyptians follow, but their chariots get stuck, and they panic. The Lord orders Moses to stretch out his hand over the sea again, and the water floods down on the Egyptians and drowns them. "And the Lord on that day delivered Israel from the hand of Egypt, and Israel saw Egypt dead on the shore of the sea, and Israel saw the great hand that the Lord had performed against Egypt, and the people feared the Lord, and they trusted in the Lord and in Moses His servant" (Exod. 14:30-31, Alter).

It's hard to read that story without wanting to stand and cheer. God has once again miraculously rescued His people, and furthermore, they now actually trust him! As in so many other points in the Exodus story, when I get to these verses I think that surely the worst is over and that after this the Israelites won't dare stop trusting God again. But how long does their trust last? Not long. In the next chapter we will see that the Israelites have new enemies to fight, and these will be even more sinister than anything Pharaoh could have thrown at them.

Questions for Reflection

1. *Do not be afraid.*
   Take your station.
   The Lord shall do battle for you.
   You shall keep still.

   Those are four commands Moses gives the Israelites as Pharaoh's soldiers approach for their attack. If you were in their shoes, which of these orders would you have the most difficulty following? Which do you have the most trouble following in your life?

2. Have you faced crisis moments when you've sensed the Lord leading you to "take your station" and "keep still" while He fights the battle for you? Describe that situation and how it worked out. What would have happened if you had fought the battle yourself instead?

3. What do you think Dan learned from those days of sitting on his couch and waiting on God for an answer?

4. What are some indications of when it may be time to act and when it may be time to "take your station" and wait on God?

Nine

PRINCIPLE 9

Know your enemies— their names are Restlessness, Complaining, and Disobedience.

GOD has wiped out Pharaoh's army. As the Israelites head toward the Promised Land, God leads them with a pillar of cloud during the day and a pillar of fire at night. Bread called manna rains down from the sky for them to pick up and eat.

Sounds pretty good, doesn't it?

And yet at this point in their story the Israelites fall into a pattern that will mar their journey for the next 40 years. It's a pattern that's familiar to many of us in our own spiritual journeys.

It's a pattern of

1. **Restlessness,** which leads to
2. **Complaining,** which leads to
3. **Disobedience,** which leads to
4. **A Longer Journey**

It's easy to think that if we had been in the Israelites' shoes, we would have handled things better. Sure, I have my own struggles with impatience at God's sluggish pace in my life, and I complain to Him and to anyone else who will listen about how I wish circumstances were different.

However, comparing myself to the Israelites, I can easily make excuses for myself. After all, unlike me, they have so many visible signs of God's leading. They *watched* that mind-boggling destruction of Pharaoh's army. They can *see* that pillar of cloud and that pillar of fire. They can pick up that manna off the ground. And still they can't trust God?

The minute they run into difficulty, they turn on Moses and Aaron as if they've never seen God do a single miraculous thing. In Exod. 16 they moan, "Would that we had died by the Lord's hand in the land of Egypt when we sat by the fleshpots, when we ate our fill of bread, for you have brought us out to this wilderness to bring death by famine on all this assembly" (Exod. 16:3, Alter). How is that for gratitude for all that God—not to mention Moses and Aaron—has done?

They have trouble obeying the simplest commands. When God rains down the manna, Moses tells them not to hoard more than what they need for each day, for God will provide it. But some of them, afraid that maybe the manna won't arrive the next day, keep it overnight anyway, and it breeds worms and stinks. They're to collect and bake an extra portion only in preparation for the Sabbath, the only day of the week when no manna falls, but some of them disobey this command, too, and find nothing when they go out on the Sabbath to gather their manna. They complain extravagantly about the water, too, even though God miraculously provides it. They eventually get tired of the manna and gripe that they want meat instead.

What's their problem?

Don't Give Me Bread and Water—Give Me the Promised Land!

Yes, the Israelites grumble about their living conditions, but are food and water really what these complaints are all about? Or could it be that the deeper frustration underlying these grievances is that they don't really want to be wandering around the desert in the first place? They want to *get there*—to Canaan, the place they thought they were headed all along.

Think of sitting in a traffic jam on the freeway. No one is happy when all those cars crawl to a stop and thinks, *Ahh— this traffic jam will give me more time to enjoy the scenery along the side of the road, to smile at other drivers, to slow down and enjoy the comforts of my car.* No, everyone I know only wants to get out of that mess and get to where he or she is headed.

Or think of an airplane ride. I don't know anyone who hopes that the airplane will taxi around the runway for two or three hours so they can watch more airplanes take off or have more time to be strapped in their seats munching a bag of pretzels. Everybody wants the plane to *take off* and reach its destination as quickly as possible.

Now imagine what it would be like to taxi around that runway for 40 years! That's exactly what Moses and the Israelites had to do. It's what many of us feel we're doing also—wandering around in a wilderness and waiting on God, our greatest dreams on hold, our prayers seemingly unanswered. We don't mean to be ungrateful for all God has done, but even manna dropped from heaven gets old after a while when all we really want is to escape this desert and get to our Promised Land.

As God leads us on this long trek, we're prey to the same dangers that so often undermined the Israelites. Disobedience leads to devastating consequences. Notice how disobedience always backfires for the Hebrews. They hoard manna so it doesn't run out, but it ends up worm-infested and stinking instead. Later in their journey, *disobedience actually makes their wait longer and ensures that some of them will never live in the Promised Land at all.* In Num. 13 Moses sends men to spy out the land of Canaan, which God is about to give them. The fulfillment of their long wait is so close! When the spies come back, they report that the land is in fact "actually flowing with milk and honey, and this is its fruit" (Num. 13:27, Alter).

However, the spies give a pessimistic slant on the report, saying that the land they scouted "is a land that consumes those who dwell in it, and all the people whom we saw in it are men of huge measure. And there did we see the Nephilim, sons of the giant from the Nephilim, and we were in our own eyes like grasshoppers, and so we were in their eyes" (Num. 13:32-33, Alter).

How do the Israelites receive this report? Do they say, *those giants may be big, but God is bigger*? Do they say, *God has worked so many miracles for us already that we can't wait to see how He'll sweep away this problem*? No, once again they turn to complaining, and they do it in the familiar hyperbolic tone: "Would that we had died in the land of Egypt, or in this wilderness would that we had died. And why is the Lord bringing us to this land to fall by the sword? Our women and our little ones will become booty. Would it not be better for us to go back to Egypt?" (Num. 14:2-3, Alter).

God is understandably furious with this response. How much more does He have to do to prove to them that He has the power to overcome all their enemies? Besides, we have seen how restless the Israelites are with this journey. Wouldn't you think they would jump at the chance to stop all this waiting and finally reach their destination, despite the dangers involved?

And yet have I not stood in that same spot? I know what God has done in the past, *but there are giants in front of me right now!* I know I've been restless and have complained nonstop that God is moving too slowly. I know that I've prayed to God repeatedly to bring me this moment, and yet—what if I fail? What if I step out and am humiliated? This whole thing is His fault anyway! He took so long to move that I've kind of gotten used to this wilderness. OK—maybe I *am* stuck in a spiritual rut. Maybe my life is *not* producing much fruit. On the other hand, at least I'm not making a fool of myself! I'm not making much progress, but the giants aren't ripping me to shreds either! Maybe I'll stay just a little longer.

Think of the times of greatest spiritual triumph in your life, when God's work in you was most evident. Don't those times usually involve a moment of stepping out in spite of fear? You feel God calling you to switch careers, or to move to a new city, or to give an amount of money for His work that is larger than what you've given before, or to take a stand for Him against injustice at work or in your neighborhood. These leap-of-faith moments might be preceded by years of waiting —"taking our station," letting God fight our battles for us—but then our own moment of truth finally comes. The wait is over. Will we take the step? Or will we turn away and cover it up with excuses such as *I'm still not ready, The obstacles are too great,* or *Maybe this was a bad idea to start with?*

After Failure—a Second Chance

The Israelites fail in their response to the report of the spies. God comes close to abandoning them, but after Moses' intervention, He decides to punish them by not allowing those over age 20 to personally enter the Promised Land. By now their story looks pretty bleak, doesn't it? And we haven't yet even mentioned some of their worst transgressions, such as when they make a golden calf to worship while Moses is up on Mount Sinai. As Durham points out, it's surprising that God does not simply wipe them out: "By every standard of ancient Near Eastern covenant making, the result of Israel's willful violation of the commitment so willingly and so solemnly made should be abandonment of the relationship, curse replacing blessing. . . . [God] is, with their violation of the terms of the covenant, under no further obligation to them. He not only *can* abandon Israel without further ado, but really *should* do so."[1]

But God does not abandon them. He gives them another chance. And another. And another. Those who disobey pay dire consequences. Even Moses does not personally get to the Promised Land because of his disobedience. But in spite of all the confusion, failure, messiness, delays, and other obstacles, God's plan prevails. God's people make it to the Promised Land. The wilderness time, though long and difficult, is not wasted. God uses the time to prepare the people, to bring them the Ten Commandments, to establish His covenant with them. As Moses sums it up in Deuteronomy 29, "And I led you forty years through the wilderness. Your cloaks did not wear out upon you and your sandal did not wear out upon your foot. Bread you did not eat, and wine and strong drink you did not drink, so that you might know that I am the Lord your God" (Deut. 29:4-5, Alter). In other words, though the wait is long, God takes care of them.

I thank God for second chances. After all, it's so easy to make a mess of things. I step out rashly when I should wait on God, and then I'm paralyzed with fear once He finally tells me to move. He could give up on me if He wanted to. Instead, He forgives, gently guides me back to the right path, and lovingly invites me back to Him.

I wish I could say that we were finished with the risks of restlessness during a long wait, but there's one final pitfall to consider in the next chapter: the danger of shortcuts.

Questions for Reflection

1. After a long period of waiting on God, our fears may make us reluctant to move once He finally opens up the oppor-

tunity to do so. We may fear the "giants" who inhabit the "Promised Land" just ahead of us. Consider the following quotation from this chapter:

I know I've been restless and have complained nonstop that God is moving too slowly. I know that I've prayed to God repeatedly to bring me this moment, and yet—what if I fail? What if I step out and am humiliated? This whole thing is His fault anyway! He took so long to move that I've kind of gotten used to this wilderness. OK—maybe I *am* stuck in a spiritual rut. Maybe my life is *not* producing much fruit. On the other hand, at least I'm not making a fool of myself! I'm not making much progress, but the giants aren't ripping me to shreds either! Maybe I'll stay just a little longer.

Have you ever fallen prey to this kind of thinking? Describe such a situation and how you worked through it. Are there other motivations besides fear that make us reluctant to move to the "Promised Land" once the doors of opportunity are opened?

2. Once the Israelites receive the pessimistic report from the spies who scouted out the Promised Land, they respond with this extravagant complaint: "Would that we had died in the land of Egypt, or in this wilderness would that we had died. And why is the Lord bringing us to this land to fall by the sword? Our women and our little ones will become booty. Would it not be better for us to go back to Egypt?" (Num. 14:2-3, Alter).

Rewrite this complaint as it might be stated by Christians today. Looking at this and similar complaints of the Israelites, do you see these attitudes in your own life or in the lives of other Christians? Is complaining contagious? What happens when it gets out of control?

3. Biblical scholar John I. Durham writes that after the disobedience of the Israelites, God is, "with their violation of

the terms of the covenant, under no further obligation to them. He not only *can* abandon Israel without further ado, but really *should* do so." Instead, God chooses not to abandon them. Discuss this concept of God's second chances. What other biblical examples of it can you think of? How much of our Christian faith hinges on this idea?

Ten

PRINCIPLE 10

Cling to God's purposes—even if you have a quicker plan of your own.

WE ALMOST never admit this, but many of us Christians believe we know better than God how to run our lives. Oh, He's competent with the big issues, like keeping the earth spinning and the sun ablaze, but as for the details of our lives, we would really rather take care of those ourselves. After all, He's a little slow sometimes, and frankly, His way of going about things is just a little weird. It's not that we want to *rebel* against God and go an entirely different direction than the way He's leading us, but we believe we can improve a little on His timing.

Some of us, having grown tired of waiting so long for an answer from God or clear direction from Him, prematurely conclude that He doesn't care about us and that we no longer need to seek His guidance on how to conduct our lives. Others who would prefer that God behave like a magical genie who instantly grants wishes refuse to accept any answer that involves a long wait, as God's methods often do. So we reject His way in favor of our own quicker solution. If we can find a shortcut to where we want God to lead us, why shouldn't we take it?

Our culture is fond of shortcuts. Lotteries are popular because people see them as a shortcut to wealth. The profusion of gambling casinos across the country is fueled by the fantasy of quick riches. This mentality is prevalent in other areas of life also. Why are crash diets so popular? Because the lure of an easy way to quick weight loss is irresistible. Why do so many people get bogged down in credit card debt? Because using a credit card is a shortcut to owning something faster than saving and waiting until they can actually afford it.

The shortcut mentality can lead to ruinous consequences. Shortcuts may take many forms. For instance, if we've been wronged and God has been too slow at setting things right, we can find our own subtle ways of exacting revenge and "setting things right." Or if we find ourselves moving too slowly in our career, and God is sitting back doing nothing, we can find ways to push ourselves ahead by whatever means necessary. In other words, we think we can speed things up a little and get to where we want to be faster than God is getting us there. Surely He won't mind if we take a little *deviation* from His plan. The fact is—He *does* mind.

Throughout history people have followed this same mentality of trying to find a quicker, easier path to God's spiritual riches than the one He has laid out. What can we learn from these people about the consequences of taking a shortcut from God's plan?

- **Sometimes our own impatience, lusts, or desires overwhelm our determination to wait on God and follow His leading.**

Esau is one of the best examples of a biblical figure who illustrates the pitfalls of sacrificing long-term benefit for short-term gratification of desire. When Esau, Isaac's oldest son, comes in from the field, he's famished. His younger brother, Jacob, has prepared a stew. Notice the strange words Esau speaks in Robert Alter's translation of this story: "And Esau said to Jacob, 'Let me gulp down some of this red red stuff, for I am famished'" (Exod. 25:30).

Red red stuff? Why does he call it that? Alter explains that "the writer comes close to assigning substandard Hebrew to the rude Esau. The famished brother cannot even come up with the ordinary Hebrew word for 'stew' (*nazid*) and instead points to the bubbling pot impatiently as (literally) 'this red red.' The verb he uses for 'gulp down' occurs nowhere else in the Bible, but in rabbinic Hebrew it's reserved for the feeding of animals."[1]

Esau is reduced to pure appetite in this story. He loses sight of everything except what will squelch his hunger *right now*. Jacob takes advantage of this weakness in his brother by offering him a deal. If Esau will sell him his birthright, he can have some stew. What a horrible idea for Esau! His birthright is his identity, one of the most valuable aspects of his life. Trade it for a bowl of stew? Surely he would never take such a foolish shortcut to the easing of his hunger pangs. Unfortunately, Esau responds, "Look—I am at the point of death, so why do I need a birthright?" He sells it and gulps down the bread and stew. He has changed his own life—and history—forever.

Selling one's birthright for a bowl of stew might sound like a remote problem in our day, but the underlying temptation is one that people now face all the time. It's what happens when someone, for instance, is waiting and praying for a relationship that will lead to a godly, Christ-centered marriage. When the wait gets too long, the person gives up and settles for whoever is at hand, even if the relationship is unhealthy. *The void must be filled now!* Or it's what happens when people don't have as much money as they want and take whatever shortcut will get them more—cheating on taxes, gambling, devoting their lives to work at the expense of family, compromising their business ethics. Or it's what happens when people fill emotional voids with quick fixes like overeating, drugs, or countless wasted hours in front of the television.

Paul vividly describes the results of the shortcut approach to life in Gal. 5. Here is Eugene Peterson's translation:

> It is obvious what kind of life develops out of trying to get your own way all the time: repetitive, loveless, cheap sex; a stinking accumulation of mental and emotional garbage; frenzied and joyless grabs for happiness; trinket gods; magic-show religion; paranoid loneliness; cutthroat competition; all-consuming-yet-never-satisfied wants; a brutal temper; an impotence to love or be loved; divided homes and divided lives; small-minded and lopsided pursuits; the vicious habit of depersonalizing everyone into a rival; uncontrolled and uncontrollable addictions; ugly parodies of community. I could go on (Gal. 5:19-21, TM).

- **Taking a shortcut to disaster: If God won't help us, we'll do it our own way.**

If you think of the greatest moments of the Old Testament, one of them would surely be Moses receiving the Ten Commandments from God on Mount Sinai. However, this episode also coincides with one of the worst examples in history of a people taking a shortcut from God's ways and disastrously pushing forward with their own evil scheme.

What a historic day when the Israelites watch Moses go up Mount Sinai! They have the incredible opportunity to witness the glory of the Lord: "And the sight of the Lord's glory was like consuming fire at the mountaintop before the eyes of the Israelites. And Moses entered within the cloud and went up the mountain, and Moses was on the mountain forty days and nights" (Exod. 24:17, Alter).

This should be one of the most thrilling times of their lives, but the problem comes with the seemingly innocuous words at the end of that verse: "forty days and nights." If they had known their leader was going to be gone that long, then they might have been able to brace themselves for the long wait. But they don't know when Moses is coming back. It could be four days or four years, for all they know. Once Moses disappears into that cloud of the Lord's glory, they're not sure exactly *what's* going on. We now know that the finger of God was writing the Law on Moses' tablets of stone, an event that would change the history of the world, but all the Israelites know is that day after day and week after week go by with no sign of Moses.

The people have only one assignment to fulfill while Moses is away. Moses tells the elders, "Sit here for us until we return to you, and look, Aaron and Hur are with you. Whoever has matters to air may approach them" (Exod. 24:14, Alter). Sounds easy enough. Just sit there! This is another "take your station" moment. All their needs are taken care of. Temporary leaders are put in place. They have only to wait.

But waiting is harder than almost any command for action they could have been given. They get restless, bored, and scared. What if Moses never comes back? Their doubts take over, and they make a terrible decision: "And the people saw that Moses lagged in coming down from the mountain, and the people assembled against Aaron and said to him, 'Rise up, make us gods that will go before us, for this man Moses who brought us up from the land of Egypt, we do not know what has happened to him'" (Exod. 32:1-2, Alter).

Instead of talking them out of this very bad idea or at least refusing to go along with it himself, Aaron tells the people to turn in their golden rings, and he molds them into a molten calf. However, he also tries to hang onto a little bit of his belief in the Lord he is betraying by declaring, "Tomorrow is a festival to the Lord" (Exod. 32:5, Alter). Not surprisingly, this festival turns from a religious ceremony into a wild, drunken party. "And they rose early on the next day, and they offered up burnt offerings and brought forward communion sacrifices, and the people came back from eating and drinking and they rose up to play" (Exod. 32:6, Alter). Alter explains that the strong implication of this wording "is a bacchanalian celebration (accompanied by food and drink) that involves shouting and song (verse 18) and dance (verse 19) and probably orgiastic activity as well."[2]

In the meantime, Moses is still on nearby Mount Sinai with the Lord carrying out some of the most important work in the history of the nation. It's easy to condemn the actions of the people, but can't many of us relate to their lack of good judgment? As we wait on God in our own lives, not aware that He's already acting, we get bored. We get scared. We worry, thinking, *What if I'm stuck here forever?* We panic. We make rash decisions. We reason, *If God's not going to work in my life, then I'll make something happen! I'll have fun, if nothing else. If holding out for meaning has failed, I'll settle for pleasure. I'll fill the void with food, shopping, money, drugs, with anything that makes those long days fly by faster.*

If I'm in college and that's taking too long, I'll drop out. If I'm building a church but it's taking too long, I'll abandon it. If I'm building relationships with people but I'm running into too much difficulty, I'll settle for superficiality.

The Israelites pay dearly for their refusal to wait. The Lord nearly decides to wipe them out, sparing them only when Moses intervenes on their behalf. Three thousand offenders are killed in the aftermath of this debacle, and God puts a scourge on the people.

We often pray for strength to accomplish difficult tasks or to handle the stress when we have too many things to do. In contrast, during those long periods of waiting on God, when "nothing" is happening, it's easy to become less vigilant. We drift. We give way to the impulses that arise from the temptations of boredom and insecurity. At some points in our lives, waiting will be as crucial as any action we've ever taken, and we'll be able to do it only when we depend completely on God's strength to keep us steady and still.

Questions for Reflection

1. This chapter tells the story of Esau, who traded his birthright for a bowl of stew. What are some modern equivalents of that kind of abandonment of long-term benefit in favor of short-term gratification? How can we guard against those temptations?

2. Do you believe the shortcut mentality is more prevalent now than in previous generations? Why or why not? What are some of the worst examples of this way of thinking in our day?

3. As the Israelites waited for Moses to come back down Mount Sinai, doubt and fear began to settle in. Little did they know the magnificent things God was doing! In your own periods of waiting on God, what doubts and fears have you been tempted to indulge? What can the experience of the Israelites teach you about those?

4. When Aaron agreed to make the golden calf for the people to worship, he tried to offset that betrayal of God by declaring a "festival to the Lord" for the next day. Do people today also try to keep a foot in both camps? In what ways? For Aaron, this attempt at having it both ways is a disaster. How does it turn out for people today?

Part 2
PERSPECTIVES ON TIME AND GOD'S TIMING

Eleven

AREN'T WE THERE YET?

**Coming to Grips
with the Nature
of Time**

"WITH GOD, one day is as good as a thousand years, a thousand years as a day. God isn't late with his promise as some measure lateness" (2 Pet. 3:8-9, TM).

Is God slow, or is He fast? What *is* slow? What *is* fast?

When I order my meal at my favorite restaurant and the waiter brings out the food ten minutes later, I think, *Wow— that was fast!*

But when I sit behind a car as the stoplight turns green, and that car doesn't move for five seconds, then ten seconds, I hit my horn and think, *What's wrong with this guy?*

Now imagine my reaction if that driver were to sit at the green light in front of me for ten *minutes.* Those same ten minutes that seemed so fast at the restaurant would seem like an eternity at the stoplight. Horns would blare. Tempers would flare. Drivers would do whatever they could to get around that car and get moving.

When we're waiting on God, do we think of Him as fast,

like the ten-minute waiter, or do we think of Him as slow, like
the ten-minute wait at the light? In both cases the ten minutes
are the same, but our perception of those minutes is radically
different. What is our perception of time, and how closely
does it align with God's perception? For those of us who per-
ceive God as slow, how would our lives improve—and our
frustration level drop—if we could adopt a perspective on
time that was more similar to His? To head in that direction,
there are a few points to consider:

- **We live in a culture tyrannized by time. Adopting
  a healthier attitude toward time will require us to
  break our addiction to going faster and faster.**

In his insightful book *In Praise of Slowness*, Carl Honore
describes the moment when he realizes his obsession with
speeding up every activity of life is out of control. As he tries to
fill up the empty minutes in an airport as he waits for his plane
to take off, he flips through a newspaper and comes across an
ad for "The One-Minute Bedtime Story." Classic fairytales
have been condensed into quick summaries, and at first this
strikes Honore as a brilliant idea. Although his two-year-old
son prefers long stories told at a slow pace, Honore always
pushes him toward shorter books and rushes through them.

> We often quarrel. "You're going too fast!" he cries. Or,
> as I make for the door, "I want another story!" Part of me
> feels horribly selfish when I accelerate the bedtime ritual,
> but another part simply cannot resist the itch to hurry on
> to the next thing on my agenda—supper, e-mail, reading,
> bills, more work, the news bulletin on television. Taking a
> long, languid stroll through the world of Dr. Seuss is not
> an option. It is too slow.[1]

As he wonders how quickly he can get the condensed
fairytales shipped to him, Honore is finally hit with the real-
ization that his mania for speed has reached an absurd level.

Can he not even slow down long enough to read a bedtime story to his son? He writes, "My whole life has turned into an exercise in hurry, in packing more and more into every hour. I am Scrooge with a stopwatch, obsessed with saving every last scrap of time, a minute here, a few seconds there. And I am not alone. Everyone around me—colleagues, friends, family—is caught in the same vortex."[2]

The drive to speed things up is so strong that even scientists have turned their attention to finding better ways to control our perception of time. One of the most frustrating wastes of time in a hurry-up culture is waiting in line. Would you believe there is actually a science devoted to this problem? It is known as the science of queuing and includes researchers in mathematics, physics, and psychology.[3] Researchers estimate that from the theater to the ballpark to the bank to the shopping mall, the average American spends two to three years in line.[4]

For experts in queue theory, the thought of all those time-obsessed Americans tapping their feet and fuming as they spend endless hours in line raises daunting challenges. For instance, how can people who can't stand to wait two minutes for a microwave dinner be persuaded to stand in a three-hour line at Disneyland for a four-minute ride? The way they do it is not to shorten the line but to change your perception of it.

How? As Martin Miller explains, "If Disney guests saw what a one-hour wait looked like in a continuous single-file line, they'd be too demoralized to enter it, research suggests. That's why the Indiana Jones ride repeatedly cuts back and forth, and turns around bends and corners to prevent guests from ever spotting the front."[5] Furthermore, signs indicate wait times along the way so that guests know what to expect. Queuing experts have also helped companies like L. L. Bean manage the waits on their call-in phone lines and companies like United Parcel Service do a better job of scheduling their flights to get packages to their destinations faster.[6] Speed is always the goal, and if wait times can't be reduced, they can at least be made less agonizing.

I understand the urgency of managing time perception. I can look at my own daily life. I constantly fight the clock. On most days it feels as if every minute is driven by work or family obligations. At the university where I teach, every minute counts as I try to squeeze all my work between dropping off my children at school in the morning and picking them up in the afternoon. I squirm in my chair as committee meetings go too long. I shake my head in frustration as students show up late to class, interrupting my tightly scheduled hour of instruction. If an unexpected phone call comes or a student shows up at my office without an appointment, I fidget through conversations even as I try to be polite. I hurry through lunch so I can get back to my office. Even casual conversations with friends get cut short as I rush off to class.

This hurried pace continues at home. My wife and I guide the kids through homework, baths, dinner, and other scheduled activities—not to mention squeezing in laundry, housework, home repairs, bill deadlines, writing deadlines, e-mails, phone calls, church obligations.

Why do we allow our lives to reach such a frantic pace? Honore argues that our culture's love of speed has turned into "an addiction, a kind of idolatry. Even when speed starts to backfire, we invoke the go-faster gospel. Falling behind at work? Get a quicker Internet connection. No time for that novel you got at Christmas? Learn to speed-read. Diet not working? Try liposuction. Too busy to cook? Buy a microwave."[7]

Beyond that, we've learned to equate a fast-paced lifestyle with success. Who are we more likely to admire—the person whose life is so full of activity and accomplishment that we can hardly understand how he or she does it all, or the person who appears not to have much going on and is content to simply hang out and enjoy life? Some people wear their hectic lifestyles as a badge of pride. Honore writes, "In our hyped-up, faster-is-better culture, a turbocharged life is still the ultimate trophy on the mantelpiece. When people moan, 'Oh, I'm so busy, I'm run off my feet, my life is a blur, I haven't got time for anything', what they often mean is, 'Look at me: I am hugely important, exciting, and energetic.'"[8]

What happens when we take this frenzied perception of time and try to impose it on our expectations of God? Will He speed up and conform to our get-on-with-it timetable? Or will *we* be the ones who will have to change?

- **It's a mistake to take our own perception of time as the norm. God views time differently than we do.**

What is time? Stuart McCready, author of *The Discovery of Time*, wrote, "After many thousands of years we are no closer than we ever were to being able to say what time is. It has no shape, no smell. It leaves no mark of its own as it passes. It has no appearance by which we can know it."[9] Physicists have their own ways of explaining time. Philosophers have other explanations. In my own life, I don't want to *define* it so much as I want to *control* it. My efforts to do so are constantly thwarted.

What is wrong with my perception of time? One problem is that the *now* takes on such a sense of urgency that I lose any sense of perspective on how the things I'm so frantically waiting for fit into the bigger picture of what God is doing. Ps. 39:5-6 says, "Oh! we're all puffs of air. Oh! we're all shadows in a campfire. Oh! we're just spit in the wind" (TM). Maybe so, but I don't *feel* like a puff of air that quickly vanishes. I feel quite solid. In fact, I feel almost *permanent*, and it feels as though what I'm waiting on God to do in my life is happening too slowly, not too fast. Ironically, even as my daily life moves dizzyingly faster, I feel ever more bogged down in waiting on God. What's taking Him so long? Honore describes a phenomenon that he labels "velocitization": "When we first drive onto a motorway, 70 miles an hour seems fast. Then, after a few minutes, it feels routine. Pull onto a slip road, brake to 30 MPH, and the lower speed seems teeth-gnashingly slow. Velocitization fuels a constant need for more speed. As we get used to 70 MPH, we are tempted to lean a little harder on the accelerator, to push the speedometer up to 80 MPH or 90 MPH or higher."[10]

Because of my own addiction to moving faster and faster in my life, I have fallen into the trap of spiritual velocitization. No matter how quickly things are moving, it never seems fast enough. I have certain expectations of how long things should take (with my career, my relationships, my health, and so on), and if God doesn't meet those, I quickly give way to worry or discouragement or blame.

Scripture teaches me to shed my flawed time perception and adopt God's attitude toward time. When Jesus addresses time perception, He sounds downright casual about time compared to my frantic attitude toward it. Jesus says, "Therefore I tell you, do not worry about your life, what you will eat or what you will drink, or about your body, what you will wear. Is not life more than food, and the body more than clothing? Look at the birds of the air; they neither sow nor reap nor gather into barns, and yet your heavenly Father feeds them. Are you not of more value than they?" (Matt. 6:25-26, NIB). There is certainly no velocitization in that attitude. In that same passage, He emphasizes the futility of trying to control time or speed things up: "And can any of you by worrying add a single hour to your span of life? . . . So do not worry about tomorrow, for tomorrow will bring worries of its own. Today's trouble is enough for today" (Matt. 6:27, 34, NIB).

Similarly, James challenges Christians to stop the arrogance and futility of trying to control time: "And now I have a word for you who brashly announce, 'Today—at the latest, to-morrow—we're off to such and such a city for the year. We're going to start a business and make a lot of money.' You don't know the first thing about tomorrow. You're nothing but a wisp of fog, catching a brief bit of sun before disappearing" (James 4:13-14, TM).

A *wisp of fog*. Notice how that echoes the other phrases we've looked at in Scripture: *Puffs of air. Shadows in a camp-fire. Spit in the wind.* We don't last long. We don't control much. What does James suggest we do in the face of the fleet-ing nature of time? He says, "Instead, make it a habit to say, 'If the Master wills it and we're still alive, we'll do this or that.' As it is, you are full of your grandiose selves. All such vaunt-ing self-importance is evil" (James 4:15-16, TM). Ouch. Not only is trying to manipulate God into following my own timetable foolish and self-defeating—it's actually evil.

In contrast, notice how freeing it is to adopt the attitude toward time that Jesus and James are urging:

Do not worry about your life.

Do not worry about tomorrow.

If the Master wills it and we're still alive . . .

It's not that we don't do the work that's set before us, but the point is we don't need to force a particular outcome in a particular timeframe. We can stop all that striving and strain-ing to meet artificial, self-imposed deadlines for the way our lives should go. Instead, trust in God's will and provision.

- **Time measurements are arbitrary. We don't have to enslave ourselves to them.**

One way to break the stranglehold of an unhealthy per-ception of time is to realize how arbitrary our ways of measur-ing time really are. When I schedule a series of back-to-back 15-minute conferences for my writing students on a particular afternoon, even one student who is five minutes late can throw off the schedule for everyone else for the rest of the day. Each minute is crucial, and my day feels chaotic when the schedule gets off track. Our semesters are composed of a set number of weeks that remains the same year after year. A class period lasts 55 minutes, and if I don't let the students out on time, they'll be late to their next classes. These time measurements become so ingrained in me, and I cling to these minutes and hours and weeks so habitually, that they begin to seem almost a part of nature.

But what *are* minutes? Or weeks? Or hours? As McCready points out,

> There is nothing written in nature that says we have to divide the day into twenty-four hours of sixty minutes with sixty seconds each. The Egyptian convention of dividing the night, and by analogy the day, into twelve hours was a matter of cultural circumstance. It reflected the fact that any given night can be so divided by the risings of these groups which the Egyptians associated with the thirty-six weeks of their administrative year. By contrast, our division of each twenty-fourth of the day into sixty minutes is a relic of a completely different system: Mesopotamian base-sixty arithmetic.[11]

Mesopotamian what? I *order my life* by those little divisions of seconds and minutes and hours. And somebody just made them up? Well, what about the days of the week? McCready writes, "Naming them after gods, the way the Romans did or the traditional languages of West Africa do, helps to make the days of the week seem like part of the furniture of the universe. But the number of days in a week is entirely a matter of choice, and the whole idea of having weeks probably reflects nothing deeper than the fact that it's handy to assign a handful of names to days in a recurring pattern."[12] Some cultures, in fact, have used a ten-day week, and others have used a four-day week. None of these measurements is fixed in nature, but is merely a matter of habit and convenience. So can I really stop living my life as if they're sacred?

Another way to break free from a narrow perception of time is to look away from my own life and view the world from a larger perspective. Look at the role time plays in nature. As I write this, the California sun is shining just outside my window. How long did it take for those beams of light to get here? According to a *National Geographic* magazine cover story on the sun, it takes only eight minutes for a sunbeam to travel 93 million miles from the surface of the sun to my eyes. However, the surface of the sun was not the start of that light beam's journey. It actually started in the sun's center. The sun is so huge that *a million earths* would fit inside it. Now let's follow the light beam from where it began as a photon in the sun's core. As Curt Suplee explains, "The solar core is so dense that a single photon, the fundamental unit of light, can't go even a fraction of a millimeter before banging into some subatomic particle, where it is scattered or absorbed and re-emitted. As a result, it can take hundreds of thousands of years for a photon to ricochet its way nearly half a million miles to the sun's surface."[13] *Hundreds of thousands of years for one beam of sunlight to reach us!* And yet, in my own life, I'm tempted to lose heart if God keeps me waiting months or even weeks for an answer to my prayers.

Evidence of God's slow, patient pace is all around us in nature. I love to stand in awe beneath the giant sequoia trees in central California. Here's how one writer described them: "It is impossible to comprehend the size of a truly giant sequoia, 3,000 years old or so, until you are underneath—head thrown back, gazing at a tree larger than the Statue of Liberty. The bark alone is 30 inches thick. Each aging behemoth assumes its own shape, a grizzled totem sculpted by gales, lightning and wildfire."[14]

I have sat beneath some of these giant trees. As huge as

they are, making me almost dizzy as I gaze up toward the tops of them, I almost expect to be able to see them growing right in front of me. Something that massive surely must be changing and expanding almost constantly. And yet, of course, I never do witness any noticeable growth or change in these trees. They're magnificent living statues, still and serene to my eyes. I could sit there all day and see no change in them. In fact, I could sit there for a year—even five years or ten years—and unless some catastrophe intervened, the trees would look pretty much the same. Real change for them is measured in centuries, not in days, weeks, months, and years, as I measure my own life.

Nature is full of processes that take so long to unfold that they reach the edge of our comprehension. How long did it take the Grand Canyon to form? How many years would it take us to travel to the farthest reaches of the galaxy? We forget the vastness of time as we wait impatiently for the elevator or wonder whether that technician on the other end of the telephone is ever going to take us off hold and actually speak to us.

We also forget time's vastness when we demand quick action from God. Job, in the midst of his tremendous suffering, came to understand how different God's perspective on time was from his own: "You don't look at things the way we mortals do. You're not taken in by appearances, are you? Unlike us, you're not working against a deadline. You have all eternity to work things out" (Job 10:4-5, TM).

- **Sometimes the wait seems so long because our vision of something is far ahead of the reality. We have no choice but to wait patiently while the reality catches up to the vision.**

Imagine that we live in a five-minute world. Our time perception is that every process should take five minutes. Whatever differs from that seems too fast or too slow.

We plant seeds in our garden, water them, and five minutes later we return to harvest the vegetables. Panic! Nothing has grown! We'll all starve!

We play tennis with a friend. She hits the ball over the net. Our response should take five minutes, right? So five minutes later, we swing at the ball. What happened? The ball is no longer there, and by that time our friend has gotten tired of waiting and has left the court, too.

We attend a ground-breaking ceremony for a new church building. We turn over a shovelful of dirt, but when we come back five minutes later, there's still no building! There's still an empty field of dirt. The church has failed! God is no longer blessing us!

These are extreme examples of the kind of thinking that many of us fall into without even realizing it. Often God gives us the gift of a vision of where He's taking us. Abraham knew God was going to make his descendants into a great nation. The Israelites knew their destination was the Promised Land. Many of us sense that God is leading us in certain directions in our relationships, our careers, and our other callings. While that vision can be helpful in keeping us focused on our purpose, problems arise when we're unrealistic about how long it will take to move from the vision to the reality. We can picture the end result so clearly that we don't understand why we can't move to it *instantly*. As we wait on God to act, we're often in the dark about the steps in the process He's following and the timing He's using to get us where we want to go. He sometimes gives us a clear picture of the beginning and the end, but not much in between.

We all know that focusing on time makes it seem to drag. When you plant a seed, you can envision the flower that will spring from it, but if you made the mistake of standing there and staring at the soil until the plant emerged, that time of waiting would feel unbearably long. When my children were small enough that they had little sense of time, they would ask repeatedly when some event they were excited about was going to happen. If the answer happened to be "five weeks," that would mean no more to them than if I said "five hours" or "five millennia." I sometimes would have to tell them to stop asking. "Don't worry," I would say. "I'll let you know when the time comes. You won't miss it."

That's good advice. As mature people in everyday situations, we understand the wisdom of not increasing our frustration by concentrating too intently on every minute in a long-term process. When I first started writing this chapter, for instance, I was suffering from a painful broken collarbone. I could envision a time when it would be back to normal. Time dragged. A day with that injury felt longer than a day without it. But I knew worrying and stewing over it would not make it heal faster. Better to put it out of my mind as much as possible and put my energies into other things. The healing process could unfold on its own.

In spiritual matters, it's easy to drop this wiser approach and revert to the "aren't-we-there-yet" attitude of a child. Sometimes my kids' frustration would turn to anger toward me. Sometimes they would declare that the thing was "never" going to happen. Since I understood time better than they did, I knew their waiting would not be in vain, but it wasn't always easy to convince *them* of that.

If God is going to make us into a certain kind of person, lead us into certain opportunities, bring particular kinds of relationships into our lives, then why doesn't He go ahead and do it? Just as when I tried to console my children over the frustration of waiting for some exciting event, there's no easy answer for us. We simply have to wait. Like Moses, who kept busy with his flocks, and like Joseph, who made the best of life as a slave and prisoner, we wait, and in its good time the answer comes.

Questions for Reflection

1. Consider the idea of "velocitization," which is examined in this chapter. As life gets faster and faster, do we begin to build up unrealistic expectations of how long things should take? How does that affect us in our relationships with friends and family? How does it affect us spiritually? How does it impact our sense of satisfaction with our lives?

2. For most of us, sitting at a stoplight for 10 minutes would be torture. Can you think of other examples in our daily lives in which waiting for any length of time immediately makes us boil over with impatience?

3. This chapter mentions processes in nature that take a very long time, such as the thousands of years it takes for a giant sequoia tree to grow or the hundreds of thousands of years it takes for a photon that starts in the sun's core to reach us as a beam of light. Can you make a list of other natural processes that take a very long time? What would happen if those processes were cut short? How does that change your perspective of your own life?

4. Examine Jesus' words in Matt. 6:25-34, in which He offers a very different perspective on time than is prevalent in our culture. What are some specific, practical ways in which we can align ourselves more closely with His attitudes toward time?

Twelve

EMBRACING THE MOMENT

How Not to
Wait Your
Life Away

OH, *how sweet the light of day,*
And how wonderful to live in the sunshine!
Even if you live a long time, don't take a single day for granted.
Take delight in each light-filled hour,
Remembering that there will also be many dark days
And that most of what comes your way is smoke.
—Eccles. 11:7-8, TM

Many of us are wishing—or waiting—our lives away.

We put so much hope on what life will be like after some future event—once I get that great job, once I graduate, once I get married, once I retire—that the day we're actually living gets lost in a frantic blur.

We spend much of our time waiting to "get it over with." My college students can't wait to get class over with so they can get to their next class. Then they want that one to end as soon as possible so they can get to their part-time jobs, and then they can't wait for those slow hours to pass so they can get back to campus to get their papers written so they can get this semester over with so they can move to the next semester so they can get college over with so they can graduate and get a job so they can endure that long enough to get a better job . . .

Think of how much of our day we spend in this "get through it" mode, as if life is really about seeing how many items on our "to do" list we can check off. And yet don't we tell ourselves it won't always be this way? Sure, our lives are future-oriented right now, but that's only because we're waiting on the *big thing* to happen. And we're also waiting to get past the *big obstacle* keeping us from the *big thing*. You know what these are in your life. The *big obstacle* might be debt, college, surgery, confusion, or enemies. The *big thing* might be financial security, a better relationship, a new home, or a promotion.

Of course, the problem is that once we knock down one obstacle, a new one or two pops up. And once we do get the *big thing* in our grasp, if we ever do, it isn't quite as satisfying as we had assumed it would be, and we already have our hearts set on the next "Once this happens . . ." The chase is on again, and we sacrifice the present for the future's hazy promise.

It's only natural to long for the promising things the future may hold, and it also makes sense to do what we can to prepare for that future rather than to expect the reality of our dreams to magically materialize. But that doesn't mean we have to sacrifice *now* for it. God may take a long time to fulfill His plan in our lives, just as He took a long time in the lives of those we've already considered, such as Abraham, Joseph, Moses, Jeremiah, and—well, just about everybody in the Bible you could mention. Did those heroes of the faith sacrifice the joy and possibilities of the present to focus solely on their future calling?

What did Moses do in those years before God appeared to him in the burning bush? Fret over why God wasn't allowing him to use his skills as a leader? No, he raised a family and tended to the work set before him. Not only was Moses not obsessed with racing to his future calling—he was actually surprised when it came. His first response was to resist, but then he moved obediently into his new role, and God brought him success. Similarly, Joseph lived fully in whatever *now* he happened to get thrust into, whether slave or prisoner or national leader, and he prospered (and also bravely faced difficulties) in every role.

How sad it would be to get to the end of our lives and think, *I never really lived my life because I was always waiting for it to happen.* The excerpt from Ecclesiastes that begins this chapter urges, "Even if you live a long time, don't take a single day for granted. Take delight in each light-filled hour" (Eccles. 11:8, TM). How can we do that? How can we keep from sleepwalking through our lives and live in a way that's passionate and fully aware?

- **Embracing the moment will mean waking up to the beauty of "wasting time" and other pleasures.**

One of my favorite poems is a simple one by Robert Bly called "Driving Late to Town to Mail a Letter":

It is a cold and snowy night. The main street is deserted.
The only things moving are swirls of snow.
As I lift the mailbox door, I feel its cold iron.
There is a privacy I love in this snowy night.
Driving around, I will waste more time.[1]

"Reprinted from *Silence in the Snow Fields*, Wesleyan University Press, Middletown, Conn., 1962, reprinted by permission of Robert Bly."

This poem celebrates small but very real pleasures—the swirls of snow, the feel of the mailbox door's cold iron, the stillness of a cold night. The question is—If we were in the speaker's shoes, would we be aware enough of the *now* to notice any of those things? Or if it was late at night and we realized we had to mail a letter, would we instead charge off in the car in a huff, annoyed at ourselves for not doing this chore earlier, or trying to fix the blame on someone else who should have done it? Would we race to the mailbox as fast as we could, irritated at any other driver who got in our way? If we paid any attention at all to the cold night, would it be to gripe about having to go out in those freezing temperatures? Would we rush back home as fast as we could and then try to forget all about that pesky little interruption to our evening?

The speaker of this poem takes the time to stop. He takes time to enjoy the pleasure of the moment. He takes time to *find* pleasure in a task in which some people would find only irritation. God has suffused our lives with small, joyful moments like this, but we miss most of them as we hurtle blindly forward, wishing only that we could go faster to get to where we're going.

I'm writing this at a time when an unusual number of celebrities are on trial or in prison. As I finished reading a newspaper article about one of them the other day, I thought, *I'm so grateful not to be in jail.* I said this to a friend, who merely laughed at what he thought was a joke. Maybe it does sound a little funny at first. It's one thing to be thankful for the things you *have*, like your family, your church, your job. But to express gratitude for bad things that have *not* happened to you? That's a little more unusual. Still, I pursued the thought further and started a list of some of the benefits I enjoy—big and small—simply by not being in jail:

I have the freedom to step outside into the sunshine whenever I choose. For that matter, I can go out in the pouring rain if I want to. When I'm outside in sunshine or rain, I can keep on walking all around the neighborhood and beyond. Or I can get into my car and go anywhere! I can see my wife whenever I like. I can play with my children every day. I can eat when I choose. I can decide the menu myself! I can have a cup of coffee any time of day or night. I can turn on the television set to whatever channel I choose. I can go to my computer and spend time on any Web site I like. I can turn on every light in the house, or I can turn them off and sit by the fireplace. I can invite friends over. I can sit alone and think. I can go to church, the store, the beach, the office, the theater, the mountains.

Making this list makes me strangely happy. I feel so free! I've never been in prison, but neither do I ever allow myself to list the joys of being free from it. Even on my most stress-filled days, my life is still filled with things that should give me pleasure if only I wake up to them.

I decided to make another list. What are the little pleasures that help get me through each day and make it more enjoyable? It feels strange at first to list some of these small, even trivial, items, but it wakes me up to the joy of this day. The beauty of my life is right now. It's not simply something I'm waiting for. Here are some of the small pleasures on my list:

• That moment in the afternoon when I look out on our front porch and see the day's mail sticking up out of the mailbox.

• Checking my e-mail and seeing a friend's name in the inbox.

• Coming home to find the light flashing on the answering machine.

• Losing myself in a good book, even if I only have a half hour or so to enjoy it.

• The first bites of a juicy, hot meal when I'm really hungry.

• That morning drive to work, joining the caravan of drivers intent on getting to the office, swigging their coffee, listening to their radios. Even if I'm dreading what I face when I reach my destination, I enjoy the sense of being part of this energetic daily procession. I am in the game.

• Reading the newspaper and eating my cereal early in the morning. The newspaper itself makes me glad I'm alive in this thrilling era in history, when anything could happen next, while the breakfast gives me the soothing sense of watching events from a slight distance, safe in my own home.

• That first cup of coffee in the early morning, which I drink by myself before my family is awake, as I sit wrapped in a blanket in my recliner, watching the news on television, waking up.

• Lunch at the outdoor café at my university. My morning classes are done, people stream around me in all directions, and I eat and relax in preparation for the afternoon work.

• Giving my daughter a piggyback ride and listening to her squeal as I lurch from side to side.

• Playing handball with my son, watching his concentration, his delight when he wins a point.

• Watching a movie with my wife in the quiet of the night, after the kids have gone to bed.

• Heading out for my morning run, falling into that familiar rhythm, not really minding how hard it's going to be, my mind following its own daydreaming path.

• The cool-off after the run, knowing that the hardest physical activity of the day is over, knowing I can eat a little dessert later without guilt.

This list could go on for pages. None of these pleasures rival the biggest moments of life, like the birth of a child, getting married, landing that dream job, and so on. But while I'm waiting for those moments, which I spend most of my life doing, these small pleasures infuse happiness into my days. A long wait is more bearable if we let ourselves enjoy the ride.

I've sat in my office on some of the worst days and thought, *I'm overwhelmed by the decisions I have to make and the tasks I have to carry out. Nothing is going the way I want it to. I'm exhausted. I'm under siege. But this cup of coffee tastes really good, and I'm going to enjoy these few moments of respite and relish every sip, and I'm going to look out at the sunshine and be grateful that I'm alive. Then I'll step back into the arena and do battle.*

My son helped teach me that pleasures are all around us. When he was three years old or so, I had a terrible time getting him from the house to the driveway and then into the car. The reason was not that he didn't want to go; he loved to go places in the car! The problem was that there were so many fascinating things to see and do *on the way* to the car. There was a ball to bounce, then a toy car to race across the floor, a book to riffle through, a porch to skip across, a wind chime to try to reach up and swat, a bug to pick up and talk to, a leaf to crumble. In the meantime, I would be hurrying him along each step of the way with barely concealed (or unconcealed) impatience, knowing that if I were alone, I would already have been in the car and on the road by now.

But eventually it dawned on me that if I were alone, I would also have missed all those fun things that so entertained my son. It didn't take long for me to learn that if we really had to get somewhere on time in the car, I would have to build in a little extra time. And if we were going somewhere that did not involve a schedule, then what was the hurry? Maybe I could bounce the ball *with* my son, or talk to his bug, or play catch for a few minutes. Reaching the destination was not the only thing that mattered. *Getting* there could be enjoyable, too.

This casual approach goes against the fast-paced American way of life that is such a part of me. The faster-is-better approach has penetrated even one of the daily pleasures that should be most relaxing—enjoying a cup of coffee. I recently read an article about the difficulty that Starbucks has had in establishing itself in Vienna, Austria. While many Americans love the idea of going to Starbucks to grab a quick and delicious cup of coffee to go, many Viennese object to what they term the "U.S. paper-cup store." Sonya Yee explains that the Viennese prefer the more traditional coffeehouses, where "the coffee is brought to the table—ideally, by a surly, tuxedo-clad waiter—on a small silver tray, accompanied by a glass of water with the coffee spoon balanced on top."[2]

At one such establishment, Café Jelinek, a sign warns customers that "whoever is in a hurry will not be served." One customer spends several days a week there writing her dissertation. She said, "You can come here, and to most of the coffeehouses in Vienna, order a coffee, sit for four or five hours, read the paper, and nobody cares."[3]

In my own life I have made a deliberate effort to try to pause throughout the day and pay attention to what surrounds me. The college where I teach is split into two campuses that are separated by a pleasant 15-minute walk in the usually sunny and mild southern California weather. Walking from one campus to another is often one of my few chances during the school day to daydream, think, reflect, pray, enjoy the sun, feel grateful for being alive that day.

I'm in a distinct minority in enjoying this walk. Few students or faculty walk from one campus to another. Many drive their cars, and many others take a campus trolley. This would make some sense if it saved time, but it doesn't. Getting in and out of the car, maneuvering through traffic, and finding a parking space eat up just as much time as the walk. The trolley is at least as slow, with time spent waiting on it to arrive and unload passengers. But driving a car or taking the trolley, which have none of the benefits of walking—such as exercise and time to think—instead offer the *illusion* of speed.

Even most of those who do walk from one campus to the other avoid at all costs the quiet contemplation that this pleasant stroll affords. It's rare to see students walking without something being pumped into their heads, whether music from headphones or a voice from a cell phone. In fact, on any campus sidewalk, the most common sight is students speaking intently into cell phones, unaware of anything else around them. It's as if a quiet walk is the scariest prospect imaginable. We must not become aware! We must not burst out of our bubbles! Aliens descending on this scene from another planet would surely think these cell phones and headphones contained some nourishing element crucial to sustaining human life.

It's not only on the college campus where people use electronic devices to cut themselves off from the life around them or from their own solitude. Merle Rubin writes, "And who are all those harried souls clutching their cell phones to their ears, whether they're driving, walking, shopping, or taking their children to the park? One can't help thinking their motto should be 'Life is elsewhere,' for they seem incapable of fully giving themselves over to whatever activity they're supposedly engaged in."[4]

Life is elsewhere. I don't want that to be my theme. My life is not in some place that can be accessed only by cell phone, and it's not in some distant future. My life is here and now. I want to be present for it. I want to live it.

Questions for Reflection

1. This chapter mentions cell phones and headphones as devices that may isolate us from our surroundings and the people around us and keep us from fully experiencing the here and now. What else distracts us from paying attention to the beauty of this moment in our lives?

2. Make a list of the small pleasures that help make your day more enjoyable, no matter what other crises you may be facing. How does that list change your perspective on the richness of your life?

3. Ecclesiastes 11 says, "Even if you live a long time, don't take a single day for granted. Take delight in each light-filled hour." What are some specific ways we can do that? Why don't we do this more regularly?

4. Think of the previous 24 hours of your life. How much of it did you spend in "just get it over with" mode? What good things about the day might you have overlooked because of that attitude?

Thirteen
STAY THE COURSE
Mastering the Discipline of Waiting

DO YOU *not know that in a race the runners all compete,*
but only one receives the prize? Run in such a way that you
may win it. Athletes exercise self-control in all things; they do it
to receive a perishable wreath, but we an imperishable one. So
I do not run aimlessly, nor do I box as though beating the air;
but I punish my body and enslave it, so that after proclaiming
to others I myself should not be disqualified.
*—*1 Cor. 9:24-27, NIB

It's easy to think of *waiting* as an enemy to be conquered.
Although we spend much of our time trying to avoid waiting, we might adopt a different attitude toward it if we realized that learning to do it well may be the key to moving us
from a Christian life characterized by frustration and disappointment to a walk with God that's infused with purpose,
discipline, and fulfillment. Consider the important part waiting plays in almost every aspect of the Christian life, including hope, faith, trust, obedience, and prayer. Throughout

Scripture waiting is described not as a passive state but as a time of preparation, training, and staying the course as we head toward the eternal prize that awaits us. As the quotation that begins this chapter illustrates, Paul was fond of athletics as a metaphor for the Christian life. Let's look at the role waiting plays in the discipline of an athlete.

In the Olympics, for instance, each *second* a runner spends on the track represents countless *hours* of practice, often spread over many years, leading up to that moment. No cheering crowds witnessed those years of struggle and preparation. The athlete was willing to *wait* through the unglorified years of practice (remembering that waiting does not equate to idleness) in order to reap the reward at the end.

One such athlete who competed in the 2004 Athens Olympics was Justin Gatlin. Here's how one reporter described the moments that preceded the most important race in this runner's career:

> First he walked the race, a slow 100-meter stroll down the straightaway of Olympic Stadium Sunday night, trying to summon his courage. Around him more than 60,000 spectators clapped in time to the rollicking Greek folk song Syrtaki, while the runners he would soon face preened, stretched, and even danced along to the blasting music. Justin Gatlin took deliberate steps on the hard, orange track, gently moving his lips. *Got to run . . . got to run . . . got to run until my heart explodes.*[1]

How long had this 22-year-old been preparing for this race? It's hard to pick a date, but perhaps age four would work. As his mother told *Sports Illustrated*, "He would never walk anywhere. He would run. And he would hurdle the fire hydrants, which in New York are about every twenty feet." In junior high, high school, and college, he competed in track events, logging countless miles and endless hours in practice and races.

Obstacles arose that threatened to end his career. In 2001

he tested positive for drugs and was slapped with a two-year ban from competition. Unfortunately, the drug was contained in medicine he had been taking for many years for attention deficit disorder. The ban was lifted after a year when his medical explanation was accepted. His challenges were not over. In 2003 he tore a hamstring, which took months to heal.

Nevertheless, he made the Olympic team and finally stood on the track in Athens, perhaps just seconds away from a medal. How did it turn out? He was not favored to win, but he crossed the finish line in only 9.85 seconds. That was just .01 second shy of an Olympic record. Even more important, it was .01 second ahead of the second-place runner. Justin Gatlin won the gold medal.

All that preparation, struggle, and waiting came down to a race that filled less than ten seconds. And after all those years, .01 second, an amount of time so tiny that it's imperceptible without precise measuring devices, made all the difference. But without the *years* of preparation, the crucial *hundredth of a second* would not have been possible.

Olympic athletes understand what we as Christians often forget: To cut short that waiting and preparation time, as we so often want to do, is to cut out the triumph. Waiting will never be our favorite aspect of the Christian life, but what do we need to know about this discipline in order to win the race that we are running as Christians?

- **Let the waiting accomplish its purpose. Just as the runner does not want to step onto the track unprepared, neither should we try to manipulate God into cutting short our time of preparation to rush us to the destination to which He is carefully leading us.**

One of the scriptures that runs through my mind more often than almost any other is James 1:2-4: "Consider it a sheer gift, friends, when tests and challenges come at you from all sides. You know that under pressure, your faith-life is forced into the open and shows its true colors. *So don't try to get out of anything prematurely*. Let it do its work so you become mature and well-developed, not deficient in any way" (TM, emphasis added).

The emphasized words are the ones that sting me in the times when I'm tempted to short-circuit God's processes and find an easy way out of the challenges that the Christian life presents. The ideas in the passage are so important that I would like to look at another translation of them also: "My brothers and sisters, whenever you face trials of any kind, consider it nothing but joy, because you know that the testing of your faith produces endurance; and *let endurance have its full effect*, so that you may be mature and complete, lacking in nothing"(NIB, emphasis added).

Don't try to get out of anything prematurely.

Let endurance have its full effect.

Consider tests and challenges a gift.

Think of trials as pure joy.

These ideas are counterintuitive. Why wouldn't we want to do just the opposite of that? It would make more sense to say, *Think of tests and trials as pure pain and get through them as quickly as you can.*

Let's go back to the Olympic runner. He would understand those statements from Scripture. He would know better than to say, "Do whatever you can to avoid workouts. Running is hard, so don't do any more than you absolutely have to. You already know how to run, so that should be enough for the big race that's coming up. Take the afternoon off and go wolf down a pizza."

If the athlete is so readily able to accept long periods of struggle and training that lead to the mastery of his skill, then why is it so much harder to accept these agonizing times of waiting and preparation in our lives as Christians? One difference is that in athletics, that time of training leads to a more easily measurable outcome—I either learn to run faster or I don't. I either beat the other runners or I don't.

With spiritual matters, the outcome is not so clear. Where is God leading us? What is the destination? As we've seen with biblical figures like Moses, Joseph, and others, God usually doesn't provide a clear road map from the beginning. We have to trust Him. We may not even know exactly what we're waiting for, just as Moses didn't know as he tended his flocks in Midian and Joseph didn't know as he languished in prison.

Often the destination to which God is leading is not a place but rather a change in character. The passage from James says to "let endurance have its full effect, so that you may be *mature and complete, lacking in nothing*" (emphasis added). What does it mean to be *mature* and *complete*? How will I know when I get there? One of the tough things about maturity is that most people think they already have it when they don't. If you don't believe me, then try to find people who will admit to being spiritually immature. I've never particularly wanted to admit it myself. So if God is asking me to endure all this waiting and difficulty to achieve a maturity I think I already have, won't it feel as if I'm waiting for no reason? How far will I be willing to submit myself to His discipline and training in order to achieve a state of being that I won't even recognize until after I've reached it? That's the kind of trust to which James is calling us. We learn to say, *Lord, I don't know why I have to go through this, but I'm willing to endure it and not try to wiggle out of it, because I trust that you're leading me to a spiritual outcome that's better than what my flawed understanding has the power to grasp right now.*

As a college professor, I know that students are not always aware of what they don't know. In other words, a mediocre student who enters my Freshman Writing Seminar may think that he or she is already an excellent writer who doesn't really need this course. Frankly, this is the most difficult type of student to work with, much harder than the student who is an even weaker writer but knows it and is willing to work hard to improve. Often the overconfident student simply never has had the kinds of writing tasks that will push him or her to the next level.

When the demands of my course challenge and stretch the student, this may be the first time he or she has been asked to do a writing assignment that isn't easy. When I go over early drafts of the work with the student, I may be marking his or her writing in ways that no other teacher ever has. This is the crucial moment for the student. Will this discomfort and criticism and suggestions make the student's work better? Will the student trust me to help bring up his or her writing a few notches? Or will my feedback and criticism be resented and turn the student to pouting or blame or resignation?

Similarly, if God has stuck us in a place we don't like, will we trust Him to lead us out in His own timing? Or will we instead hatch our own faster scheme the way the Israelites did when they urged Aaron to make a golden calf for them to worship instead of waiting for Moses to complete his work on Mount Sinai? If we're facing difficulties that are building patience in us or that are breaking down our selfishness to make us more caring, will we submit to that? Or will we instead resist and turn to attitudes in the opposite direction—bitterness, cynicism, self-centeredness, grasping whatever we can get on our own terms?

- **As in any long-distance race, we Christians will hit many times when we feel like quitting. What can we do to make sure we make it to the finish line?**

Several mornings a week I run a few miles for exercise. I've done this for so many years that you might think I would be used to it by now and would have stopped trying to talk myself out of it. However, on many mornings I find myself trying to think of excuses not to run. *Maybe this would fit into my schedule better later in the day*, I tell myself, knowing deep down that if I don't do it first thing, I won't do it at all. *Maybe my body is telling me that a run today would be too strenuous*, I say, knowing in reality that my body is saying no such thing. It's amazing how many reasons I can come up with to avoid doing the thing I really want to do, which is running.

I know that in running, consistency is the most important element. I run to stay healthy and keep my weight down, and that won't happen if I run one day and then take the next three weeks off before I run again. When I'm out there following my usual route, I see many of the same people day after day. We wave and speak an encouraging word to one another. Occasionally somebody new pops up. I sometimes try to predict how long that person will last. How could I possibly tell? One clue, oddly enough, is how elaborate the person's running gear is. Are there headphones, sweatbands, new shoes, a crisp new cap, an unwrinkled warm-up suit that matches? If so, then chances are that after about a week or so I'll never see that person out running again.

The regulars long ago gave up caring how they look when they run. They wear the same old battered outfits. They don't need to be entertained as they run. They're out in all kinds of weather. They never quit until their route is finished. They stay the course. They don't get off track.

I've seen some of these tendencies displayed in other long-term endeavors. I entered a doctoral program in American literature knowing that only about half of those who enter such a program end up with the degree. The half who made it were not necessarily the ones I would have predicted when we first entered the program. Those who made it were not always those who gave the most dazzling answers in class discussions or who were the focus of attention at weekend parties. Many of those who flashed so brightly at first were the ones who fizzled out the fastest. I remember how stunned I was when I watched people who I knew were smarter than I burn out or flunk out.

I eventually realized that finishing a doctoral program takes stamina more than anything else. It takes a certain level of knowledge and intelligence to get into such a program, of course, but after that, success depends upon the person's willingness to carefully and consistently finish the coursework, prepare for and take the exams, conduct meticulous research, and sit at the computer day after day, month after month, until the dissertation is written. Why did so many bright people fail? The qualities that made them able to rattle off a few brilliant paragraphs in class were not the same characteristics that would empower them to sit through the lonely, sometimes discouraging hours at the computer trying to make sense of a pile of research. They got off track. They did not stay the course.

How many people who enter a doctoral program at some point think they want to quit? Almost everyone. I can't think of anyone I knew in graduate school who didn't seriously contemplate quitting at some point. I know I did. In the early stages of writing my dissertation, the idea popped into my head to abandon the project, move to New York City, and start a new career in journalism. I knew no one in New York. I had no job prospects there. Nevertheless, I started subscribing to the Manhattan edition of *The New York Times* and checked the want ads every day.

It was not a well-thought-out plan. It didn't make much sense for me, so before long I canceled my *Times* subscription and got back to work on the dissertation. Why? Because the joy of the work I was immersed in returned. I remembered that I really did love reading and writing about literature. I really did want to be a college professor and spend my life teaching students about these great authors. Before I finished the degree, I had other moments of doubt, but I stayed the course, and I'm glad I did. To this day I'm still benefiting from that decision. The path was not smooth, and I wasn't always happy to be on it, but it got me where I wanted to go.

Let's face it. No matter how deeply we love the Lord, there are times we want to stray from the Christian path. Like the runner with the headphones and sweatband and designer jogging outfit, we start with good intentions, loving the benefits of the Christian life—the exhilaration of God's spirit in our lives, the assurance of salvation, the love of fellow believers, the beauty of worship, the truth of Scripture. Like the first-year graduate student, we enter the faith determined never to stray. Why would we want to? We believe our faith is so strong we'll never waver.

But eventually something happens that threatens to knock us off this path. It may come in many forms. A tragedy such as the death of a loved one or a terrible illness or disability may make us question whether God really exists or really loves us. We may be tempted by a sin so alluring that we can barely control ourselves from chasing after it. We may get worn down or discouraged by goals and dreams that go unfulfilled because it seems as if God is ignoring our prayers. We may simply start to *drift* off the path of faith while barely being aware we're doing so.

Is this temptation to get off course unavoidable? I believe it is. I believe God can help prevent us from actually straying off the Christian path, but I don't know of anyone who makes it through life without a time of crisis—or perhaps many such times—when he or she must make a decision. One reason I believe this is that there are dozens of times in Scripture when this issue is confronted. I have a file stuffed with Scripture references that deal with some version of the message "Stay the course."

Here's a small sampling: "Let us hold fast to the confession of our hope without wavering, for he who has promised is faithful" (Heb. 10:23, NIB). "*Hold to the standard* of sound teaching that you have heard from me, in the faith and love that are in Christ Jesus. *Guard the good treasure* entrusted in you, with the help of the Holy Spirit living in us" (1 Tim. 1:13-14, NIB, emphasis added). "*Do not, therefore, abandon that confidence of yours*; it brings a great reward. *For you need endurance*, so that when you have done the will of God, you may receive what was promised" (Heb. 10:35-36, NIB, emphasis added). "*But we are not among those who shrink back* and so are lost, but among those who have faith and so are saved" (Heb. 10:39, NIB, emphasis added). "I solemnly urge you: proclaim the message; *be persistent whether the time is favorable or unfavorable*; convince, rebuke, and encourage, with the utmost patience in teaching" (2 Tim. 4:1-2, NIB, emphasis added). "*So we do not lose heart.* Even though our outer nature is wasting away, our inner nature is being renewed day by day" (2 Cor. 4:16, NIB, emphasis added). "With my whole heart I see you; *do not let me stray* from your commandments" (Ps. 119:10, NIB, emphasis added).

This list of "don't get off track" scriptures could go on for pages. Of course, it's fine to tell someone to hold steady, but if going off course is such a big risk in the Christian life, then what can we do to make sure that doesn't happen? What does that stack of scriptures have to say about how to avoid such a failure?

- **Strip away all distractions, and focus all your energy on the goal of following Him regardless of the changing circumstances that surround you.**

A time of waiting on God should not be a time of drifting. If we allow our faith and our actions to fade in and out according to the difficulties we face, then we'll spend our whole lives getting knocked off course and flailing around spiritually. After giving an overview of the lives of the heroes of faith in Heb. 11, the writer begins the next chapter with "Therefore, since we are surrounded by so great a cloud of witnesses, let us also lay aside every weight and the sin that clings so closely, and let us run with perseverance the race that is set before us" (Heb. 12:1, NIB).

What kinds of "weight" and clingy sin might he be referring to? One answer might be found in Col. 3, which calls on Christians to "set your mind on things that are above" and "put to death" things like "fornication, impurity, passion, evil desire, and greed (which is idolatry)" (Col. 3:1, 5, NIB). I'm sure we could also think of many other items to add to this list of "weights" that keep us from running a focused, purposeful race: comparing ourselves to others, lack of acceptance of God's timing and methods, resentment because of bad things that have happened to us, laziness, anger, selfish ambition.

God will help us get rid of these weights, even though His way of doing it will often be unpleasant. Hebrews says, "Endure trials for the sake of discipline. God is treating you as his children; for what child is there whom a parent does not discipline? If you do not have that discipline in which all children share, then you are illegitimate and not his children" (Heb. 12:7-8, NIB). That is not what I want to hear! I didn't like being disciplined when I was a kid, and I sure don't like it now. Couldn't God come up with a better way of teaching me? Do I really need trials? Why can't He just tell me what to do, and I'll do it?

My own children have probably asked the same question about me. In some cases, a word of advice to them has been enough, but at other times discipline has been the only means to teach them things that are absolutely crucial to their upbringing, sometimes even to their very survival. They never like it. They never thank me for it. But someday they'll understand that they're better off for it. Hebrews says, "Now, discipline always seems painful rather than pleasant at the time, but later it yields the peaceful fruit of righteousness to those who have been trained by it" (Heb. 12:11, NRSV).

With what kinds of trials does God discipline me? Sometimes He withholds things I desperately want—a certain job, a particular relationship, money, and so on—because those things would get me off track in ways I can't visualize at the moment. Sometimes He lets me go through painful experiences—persecution, health problems, job challenges—because those incidents will teach me virtues I need, such as humility, a more caring attitude toward others, a deeper reliance on God. When I endure this discipline, *I'm not off track spiritually*, even though I may be tempted to think so. I may be tempted to wonder, *Why is God not blessing me? Why is He not rescuing me? Why is He punishing me? In fact, God may be doing His most important work in me that He has ever done.* The writer of Hebrews concludes his section on discipline by saying, "Therefore lift your drooping hands and strengthen your weak knees, and make straight paths for your feet, so that what is lame may not be put out of joint, but rather be healed" (Heb. 12:12-13, NIB).

Not all discipline is imposed on us from the outside. We've also been given the power to impose discipline on our own actions. As Paul declares in the verses I quoted at the beginning of this chapter, "Athletes exercise self-control in all things; they do it to receive a perishable wreath, but we an imperishable one. So I do not run aimlessly, nor do I box as though beating the air; but I punish my body and enslave it, so that after proclaiming to others I myself should not be disqualified" (1 Cor. 9:25-27, NIB). Like a runner who undercuts his or her own training by stuffing himself or herself with chocolate bars and ice cream after a run, what do you tolerate in your life that deep down you know is slowing you down or distracting you? Watching too much television or the wrong kind of television? Neglecting prayer? A sour attitude toward your family or fellow workers? A lack of integrity in some area of your life that you've allowed to remain because you can get away with it?

Strip those things away, says Paul. Let yourself experience the sometimes severe joy of running the disciplined race.

- **Allow other Christians and heroes of the faith to serve as your role models and encouragers as you endure the long race.**

In my long race through graduate school, one of the things that made the journey more bearable and more enjoyable was going through it with my friends. We studied together, encouraged each other, shared our fears and insecurities with one another, and celebrated when we made it to the finish line. Thank God that in the race we're running as Christians, we have teammates. Most of those fellow runners are right around us — our fellow church members, small-group members, fellow Christians at our workplaces, and Christian family members. These other members of our team play a crucial role in keeping us on track and helping us have the courage to stay steady in the discipline of waiting.

Part of our own responsibility is to encourage the other runners around us. Gal. 6:2 says, "Bear one another's burdens, and in this way you will fulfill the law of Christ" (NIB). We're in direct relationship with most of these teammates, but sometimes they might be people we're seeing from a distance, such as a fellow church member we don't know well but who inspires us as we witness the grace and fortitude with which he confronts a crisis in his life. Others may be watching us even though we're unaware of it. What will they learn from us about how we run our race?

We also have other less visible teammates who are cheering us on. They're the Christians who finished the race before us and in whose footsteps we now run. James urges, "Take the old prophets as your mentors. They put up with anything, went through everything, and never once quit, all the time honoring God. What a gift life is to those who stay the course! You've heard, of course, of Job's staying power, and you know how God brought it all together for him at the end. That's because God cares right down to the last detail" (James 5:10-11, TM).

As we'll see in the next chapter, our story is not ours alone but is tied to those who went before us and those who will come after us. The race we run now might ripple into the lives of fellow believers in future generations in ways we never dreamed.

With so much at stake, it becomes easy to answer the question, *Is all this waiting and discipline worth it?* Paul, who suffered prison and torture for following Christ, told Timothy that the gospel message was "the cause of all this trouble I'm in. But I have no regrets. I couldn't be more sure of my ground—the One I've trusted in can take care of what he's trusted me to do right to the end. So keep at your work, this faith and love rooted in Christ, exactly as I set it out for you. It's as sound as the day you first heard it from me" (2 Tim. 1:11-13, TM).

Questions for Reflection

1. This chapter quotes a passage from James 1 that urges readers, "So don't try to get out of anything prematurely." What are some ways in which Christians try to wiggle out of tests and challenges prematurely? What are the dangers of that?

2. Are most Christians more impatient in their spiritual lives than in other endeavors, like athletics, that require long times of training and stamina? If so, why? What are ways that Christians can transfer an understanding of the "disci-

pline of waiting" from areas like sports into their spiritual lives?

3. Think of the time when you were most tempted to quit the race of the Christian life. Why did you want to quit? What finally kept you on course or got you back on course?

4. Make a list of the distractions that are most likely to knock you off track in your Christian journey. What steps can you take to eliminate them or minimize their effect?

Fourteen

CASTING OFF THE BOUNDARIES OF TIME

How God's Desires for Our Lives May Reach Farther Than We Ever Dreamed

WHEN MY LIFE gets bogged down with frustration because of God's apparent slowness to act, when I'm disappointed or confused by His timing and methods, it helps to remind myself of a principle that Scripture constantly keeps at the forefront: *The work God begins in me may be completed by other people. The work began in other people may be completed in me.*

I usually think of God's plan for me in purely individual terms—*my* life, *my* marriage, *my* career—and I assess God's activity, or lack of it, by that individualistic standard. To a certain extent, that's a valid way of looking at things. It's true that God has a plan for my salvation as an individual, and there's certain work He calls me to personally. However, the story doesn't stop there. In ways I can never fully know, He also makes me part of the stories of people around me. Beyond that, He intertwines my story inextricably with those of His followers from generations that went before me and with those who will come after me. If I evaluate my life only in terms of what I see in *my life*, I'm missing the full magnitude of God's work through me. *Even on what appears to be my slowest, most unproductive, most frustrating day, my life may be having an impact beyond what I ever dreamed.* How is this possible?

Compared to those who lived in Old and New Testament times, most of us give little thought to generations other than our own. Think, for instance, of all those genealogies in Scripture. How many of us could trace our lineage back that many generations? Some people put a special effort into tracing their ancestors, but in our day it does take that extra effort, since for most of us, knowledge of our ancestry is not a routine part of our family lives.

Or think of how we view our careers. In our culture there are some family businesses or professions that pass down through the generations, but for most people, one's career is an individual choice that has no particular connection to the work the previous generation did or that the next generation will do. My father worked for a division of General Motors for 40 years and now works part-time as a business consultant. I respect and admire his work, but I don't see my own work as any kind of continuation of his. I'm a writer and a professor living 2,000 miles away from his work world, and those worlds never intersect. With my own children, I have no expectation that they will pursue careers that have any connection to my own. I expect them to pursue their own interests and callings.

When we write our résumés, or when people ask us about our work, most of us would start with our first job and stop with our current job or our retirement. I wouldn't think to list the grocery store my grandparents owned or to include the accomplishments I hope my children will someday achieve. On a résumé those items would be considered irrelevant. I also wouldn't include the time I spent praying for a close friend to achieve the dreams of his own calling or the time I spent listening to him and giving him feedback as he outlined his vision of what he wanted to accomplish. When my supervisors evaluate my performance, none of those extraneous issues would count for anything either. My work is my work, and other people's work is theirs alone.

In such an individualistic age, it's hard to fully grasp one of the conclusions the writer of Hebrews comes to at the end of chapter 11, the "faith chapter." After reviewing the lives of people like Abraham, Moses, and others, he speeds through the experiences of other heroes of faith whose stories he does not have time to tell in full. Through faith these people conquered kingdoms, administered justice, obtained promises, shut the mouths of lions, quenched raging fire, escaped the edge of the sword, won strength out of weakness, became mighty in war, and put foreign armies to flight. Women received their dead by resurrection. Others were tortured, refusing to accept release, in order to obtain a better resurrection. Others suffered mocking and flogging and even chains and imprisonment. They were stoned to death, sawn in two, killed by the sword; they went about in skins of sheep and goats, destitute, persecuted, tormented—of whom the world was not worthy. They wandered in deserts and mountains and in caves and holes in the ground. (See Heb. 11:33-38).

What an astonishing chronicle of faith! Yet those brave deeds of sacrifice are not what amaze me most. Look at what comes next: "Yet all these, though they were commended for their faith, did not receive what was promised, since God had provided something better *so that they would not, apart from us, be made perfect*" (Heb. 11:39-40, NIB, emphasis added). Eugene Peterson paraphrases this passage, "Not one of these people, even though their lives of faith were exemplary, got their hands on what was promised. God had a better plan for us: that their faith and our faith would come together to make one completed whole, their lives of faith not complete apart from ours" (TM).

The lives of these great men and women of faith are not complete apart from our lives? If that's more than simply a rhetorical flourish, if we're really supposed to take that seriously, then it has huge implications for how we'll view God's work in our lives. I'm connected to Moses. I'm connected to Abraham. My story helps to complete the stories of Noah and Isaac and Gideon and David. My story—my career and calling—is not simply what I could put in a résumé between the time I graduate from high school and the time I retire. I'm part of something much bigger, and the only way to properly evaluate what God is doing in my life is to see how it fits into the big picture. In other words, if I confine my vision of how God is working in my life only to those experiences that happen to *me*, I may miss the significance of my life entirely. If my life is really only a piece of a larger whole, then it won't make complete sense if I look at it in isolation.

That sounds nice, but what difference does it really make in how I live from day to day? Is this anything more than the usual "we're all in this together as a team" verbiage? If our lives as Christians really are connected to God's followers of other generations, then how does that play out? Let's look at some examples.

Completing the Work of Others: Moses and Joshua

Moses, Elijah, David, and Paul lived some of the most exciting and significant lives in Scripture and history. Yet their stories—their vision and calling—were not completed in their own lifetimes. Crucial aspects of their vision were brought to fruition only after their deaths, by the people who followed them. Moses' mission is not complete without Joshua. Elijah's story is not fulfilled without Elisha. David's vision for the Temple is incomplete without Solomon. Paul's ministry is not complete without Timothy. These men who followed their mentors were not just *successors* pursuing their own agendas, as happens, for instance, when a new president of the United States is elected to replace the old one. These men knew they were part of the *same work* as those who went before them, and the people of both generations were aware that the significance of their own lives could not be measured individually.

As we've seen in earlier chapters, from the time God calls to Moses from the burning bush, the entire thrust of Moses' mission is to get the Israelites to Canaan. God works through him in astonishing ways to bring this about, and Deut. 34:10-12 heaps praise on Moses, declaring, "Never since has there arisen a prophet in Israel like Moses, whom the Lord knew face to face. He was unequaled for all the signs and wonders that the Lord sent him to perform in the land of Egypt, against Pharaoh and all his servants and his entire land, and for all the mighty deeds and all the terrifying displays of power that Moses performed in the sight of all Israel" (Deut. 34:10-12, NIB).

Who wouldn't be thrilled with that assessment of one's life? And yet Moses is not allowed to complete his mission. Although he leads the people through the desert for 40 years, a journey complicated and lengthened by sin and disobedience, God does not allow Moses to lead the people into the Promised Land himself. He lets Moses get tantalizingly close, sending him up to the mountain from which he can see the land. He tells Moses that he "shall die there on the mountain that you ascend and shall be gathered to your kin, as your brother Aaron died on Mount Hor and was gathered to his kin; because both of you broke faith with me among the Israelites at the waters of Meribath-kadesh in the wilderness of Zin, by failing to maintain my holiness among the Israelites. Although you may view the land from a distance, you shall not enter it—the land that I am giving to the Israelites" (Deut. 32:50-52, NRSV).

Despite Moses' own share of responsibility for not being allowed into Canaan, it's easy to see how someone else in his position might have let God's decision breed resentment and bitterness. Moses might have said, "I've led these people for 40 years through every kind of crisis! How can you possibly deny me the fulfillment of this dream by keeping me just outside the land of milk and honey?" Someone else in Moses' shoes might have *resented* the successor who would be given the privilege to lead the people to this triumph. He might have said, "Why should Joshua enjoy this crowning achievement when *I've* done all the work?" He might have worked to subtly undermine his successor so that the new man would not overshadow him. He might have tried to get the people to adopt a sense of grievance against the new leader or even against the Lord.

Most of us encounter those same temptations at some points in our lives. Let's face it. When we're waiting on God to act in our lives and pleading with Him to let us fulfill a certain role, there are few things as discouraging as watching someone else flourish in that assignment instead. Yet this will happen. Will our response be to grind our teeth in disgust at God's decision not to give us the role to which we feel entitled?

We can interpret the situation as failure, or, like Moses and Joshua and other biblical heroes, we can gratefully fulfill the assignment God has given us. We can learn to regard the others who share roles in this story not as competitors who beat us out but as teammates playing a crucial part in our larger victory. This will not be easy to do in moments of disappointment or times when selfish ambition flares up, but God can bring us contentment in our part of His thrilling story if we trust His direction.

In some episodes of our lives we may be Moses. In others

we may be Joshua. In still others we may be one of the anony-
mous Israelites who do the crucial work of waiting for the
command and then taking possession of the land. The problem with many of us comes when we want to be Moses,
Joshua, and the people all rolled into one, and if God doesn't
assign us all those roles, we think He has let us down.

Moses does not use his disappointment as an excuse to undermine the man who will lead the Israelites into the Promised
Land. Instead, he does everything he can to make sure that the
mission continues uninterrupted. He levels with the people
and reassures them: "I am now one hundred twenty years old. I
am no longer able to get about, and the Lord has told me, 'You
shall not cross over this Jordan.' The Lord your God himself
will cross over before you. He will destroy those nations before
you, and you shall dispossess them. Joshua also will cross over
before you, as the Lord promised" (Deut. 31:2-3, NIB).

Moses makes it clear that the journey is not about himself,
or even about Joshua. *The Lord* is the one who is leading
them. Moses has taken them part of the way, and Joshua will
take them the rest of the way. In front of all the people,
Moses says to Joshua, "Be strong and bold, for you are the
one who will go with this people into the land that the Lord
has sworn to their ancestors to give them; and you will put
them in possession of it. It is the Lord who goes before you.
He will be with you; he will not fail you or forsake you. Do
not fear or be dismayed" (Deut. 31:7-8, NIB). In that speech
Moses connects his own mission to the generations who went
before him (the "ancestors") and to the generation after him
(Joshua). His words gave no hint of grievance but rather reas-
surance and fulfillment.

David and Solomon: One Prepares, the Other Builds

Like Moses, David has a big vision. First Chronicles 17:1-2
says, "Now when David settled into his house, David said to the

prophet Nathan, 'I am living in a house of cedar, but the ark of the covenant of the LORD is under a tent.' Nathan said to David, 'Do all that you have in mind, for God is with you'" (NRSV).

What David wants to do is build a Temple. However, God has a different idea. Although He makes David the powerful promise that his throne will continue forever through his descendants, He nevertheless declares that David will not be the one to build the Temple. Instead, the Lord appoints David's son Solomon, whom David calls "young and inexperienced" (1 Chron. 22: 5, NIB), to build it. Being blocked from building this Temple himself must have been a big disappointment for David. After all, it was *his* dream, *his* idea, not Solomon's. He later tells Solomon, "I wanted in the worst way to build a sanctuary to honor my God. But God prevented me" (1 Chron. 22:7, TM). Although David is barred from building the Temple, he is not restricted from assisting his son with the preparations. But would he want to? Considering his son's youth and inexperience, would it be tempting for David to think, *Why should I be assisting him instead of him assisting me?*

It's easy to think of many ways David could have resisted God's plan. He could have outright disobeyed and built the Temple himself. He was king! Who would stop him? Or he could have tried to satisfy God's restriction in some legalistic way that still allowed him to pursue his own agenda, such as putting Solomon in charge in name only while really running the show himself. Or, disappointed and angry that God had chosen Solomon for this task, David could have washed his hands of the project entirely, saying, *If He wants Solomon to build it, then let him build it.*

David doesn't do any of those things. Instead, he throws all his energy into the partial role he has been given. First, he does everything he can to provide the plans and building materials Solomon will need. This includes 3,775 tons of gold,

37,750 tons of silver, and an untold number of tons of bronze, iron, timber, and stone. (See 1 Chron. 22:14, NIB.) Second, like Moses with Joshua, David does everything he can to fill his son with courage for the work ahead: "Be strong and of good courage, and act. Do not be afraid or dismayed; for the Lord God, my God, is with you. He will not fail you or forsake you, until all the work for the service of the house of the Lord is finished" (1 Chron. 28:20, NIB). Third, like Moses with Joshua, David gathers together the leaders of the nation to make it clear to them that he fully believes that God has chosen Solomon for this task and that they should support him. Furthermore, he urges the people to give offerings for the Temple, as he has done.

David will not live to see the Temple finished, but he is content to play his part. He humbly acknowledges that whatever is accomplished, whether carried out by himself or Solomon, ultimately comes from God: "O Lord our God, all this abundance that we have provided for building you a house for your holy name comes from your hand and is all your own" (1 Chron. 29:16, NIB). He understands that he is one link in the chain of generations, and like Moses, he willingly pours himself into a task whose completion someone else will have the joy of celebrating: "O Lord, the God of Abraham, Isaac, and Israel, our ancestors, keep forever such purposes and thoughts in the hearts of your people, and direct their hearts toward you" (1 Chron. 29:18, NIB).

If we choose to serve God the way Moses and David did, with the distinct possibility that some of our hardest work and fondest visions will be brought to fruition not by us but by someone else, our ego may face a severe challenge. Our lives will not be about "taking credit" for achievements that are ours alone. We won't evaluate our lives according to our own amazing feats or the various types of empires we've built. On the other hand, living this way takes the pressure off. We realize that life is not about impressing God by building some imposing personal spiritual résumé. It's about fulfilling our part in the drama He is directing and letting Him take care of the outcome.

Ripple Effect: Even When It's Over, It Isn't Over

As a college professor, I find that my life is broken up into semesters, but when does a semester end? After the students have completed their final exams? After I've turned in final grades? After everyone has gone home for break? Those used to be the markers that indicated my classes were drawing to a close, but now I realize that the semester really never ends. Class is often still in session years after I have dismissed it.

How can that be?

I've been in teaching long enough that I occasionally run into students who were in my class years ago. They often say, "I remember when you told us . . ." and then they recount some comment or idea that was meaningful to them. Sometimes I don't remember even teaching what they're telling me about, but for them it was a turning point in their thinking on that issue. Others have told me that a book I assigned or recommended got them started reading an author who was still influencing them to that day. Others have said that a job I helped them get—which I sometimes don't even recall doing—was a key step in their career.

For every student who comes back to tell me things like this, how many more must there be that I never hear about? When I think back to some of those turning points in my own life as a college student, I realize that in most cases the professors who influenced me were not aware of it.

What difference does this make to me in the present? It helps me to know that even when I'm experiencing a teaching day in which it feels as though nothing I'm saying or doing is getting through to anyone, *words I spoke to someone 10 years ago may be hitting them that very moment, just when they need it.* And even though I may look at the class I taught an hour ago and think that most of the students were resistant to the lesson, in some student's mind a seed may have been planted that may take five or ten years to bear fruit, long after I'm around to witness it.

When we consider what God is doing in our lives, one of the biggest mistakes we make is to judge our lives only on what we can *see*, and only on what we can see *now*. But there's a ripple effect that's crucially important but hard to evaluate. Think, for instance, of the money you give to the ministries of your church or to missions organizations. You give it and then move on. You don't trace what happens with each dollar. When that money allows a clinic to be opened or a Bible study to be taught or the gospel to be preached from a pulpit thousands of miles away, you will not be aware of it. At the moment someone's life is being changed, you might be thinking, *My finances are a mess. I wish I had invested my money more wisely.* In fact, you may have already made the most important financial investment of your life without realizing it.

As you wait on God to finally get moving and open up some doors of opportunity so you can start fulfilling your dream, perhaps you assist in a children's Sunday School class just to help out a friend. You might lead a child toward Jesus in ways you never become aware of. That assignment you don't even really consider part of your life's work might be the most important work you do all year. I know this, because I became a Christian during a Vacation Bible School when I was eight years old. In the midst of all the chaos, Kool-Aid, religious soap carvings, and Popsicle-stick crosses, I met Jesus. I remember the pastor who preached the message at the end of that week, but I don't remember the names of any of the workers who taught me or prayed with me. I can't name them, but I'm forever grateful for them.

I also remember my fourth-grade Sunday School teacher, who gave me a Bible after I memorized six verses of Scripture. I still have that Bible. I still remember the verses! She had a big impact on my spiritual growth, but did she take on that assignment having any idea she would make such a difference in the life of a spiritually hungry boy?

The work we do for God ripples through the generations that follow us. At my university I teach literature to many students who plan to be teachers. They in turn will pass on some of what they've learned in my classes to their own students. When I prepare one class session, how many hundreds of people might some of that work ultimately reach?

I attend church in a building that was already standing when I first went there. The pastors were already in place. Sunday School classes were already established. The congregation was already busy worshiping God and serving people and enjoying each other's friendship. Thank God, I didn't have to start the whole enterprise from scratch. I simply had to show up and find a place to fit in. The generation that built the church never knew I would end up there to benefit from it. I can be Joshua to their Moses, I can be Solomon to their David, even though I don't even know their names. As I fulfill my assignment in that place, I wonder what I may be putting in place that later generations may benefit from. I ask God to expand my vision, or at least my trust, to know that He may be doing more in my life than I ever thought possible.

Questions for Reflection

1. This chapter discusses the ripple effect of our lives—how something we do today may bear fruit years from now in ways we'll never know. List five deeds in your life—from money you've given to church to Sunday School classes you've taught to relationships you've had—that may have had ripple effects long afterward. Speculate on what those

effects might have been and might still be. How does that change your perspective on how God is working in your life?

2. What if Moses and David had viewed their roles in God's story only in individualistic terms? Write an alternative history for these men that shows what might have happened if they had rejected any plan from God that did not allow them to lead the people into the Promised Land or build the Temple *themselves*. What can we learn from this in our own spiritual lives?

3. Can you think of ways in which you're fulfilling the vision of generations of Christians who went before you? How about in your church? Your family? Your work?

4. Much of this chapter challenges the temptations of selfish, individualistic ambition. How big a problem is ambition among Christians today? Does ambition ever serve a positive function? What are its dangers?

Fifteen

GOD HAS ALL THE TIME IN THE WORLD— AND MORE

An Eternal Perspective on Waiting

THE CREATED WORLD *itself can hardly wait for what's coming next. Everything in creation is being more or less held back. God reins it in until both creation and all the creatures are ready and can be released at the same moment into the glorious times ahead. Meanwhile, the joyful anticipation deepens.*

—Rom. 8:19-23, TM

What are we waiting for?

Most of us rarely lift our eyes above the concerns of this life. We may *believe* in an afterlife, but because we know death is the only way to get there, we don't like to think about it too much. Heaven is also hard for us to picture, so it's much easier to keep our attention on the more familiar world around us.

We figure heaven can take of itself. In the meantime, we have problems to work through and dreams to fulfill right here.

The early Christians of the New Testament didn't put eternity on a shelf the way we do. For them, waiting for eternity was not simply a hazy wish for a future over which they had no control. Instead, they brought eternity into their daily lives. What can we learn from their perspective?

- **Our connection to heaven does not begin after death. It has already begun. Heaven is not separate from God's earthly plan for our lives; it is the culmination of it. His plan for us here makes no sense without heaven.**

A sense of longing, a sense of waiting, is built into us because we were never intended to achieve ultimate fulfillment in this world. That longing never goes away, no matter what we try to do to quench it. In 2 Cor. 5:2 we're told, "For in this tent we groan, longing to be clothed with our heavenly dwelling" (NIB). Or as Peterson translates part of this chapter, "Compared to what's coming, living conditions around here seem like a stopover in an unfurnished shack, and we're tired of it! We've been given a glimpse of the real thing, our true home, our resurrection bodies! The Spirit of God whets our appetite by giving us a taste of what's ahead. He puts a little of heaven in our hearts so we'll never settle for less" (2 Cor. 5:3-4, TM).

In our day many Christians feel uncomfortable thinking too much about heaven, as if doing so somehow means they're avoiding dealing with the "real world" of the present. But for early Christians, thoughts of heaven and thoughts of the second coming of Jesus were not *avoidance* of the present; instead, these thoughts were a way of keeping the present in its proper perspective. Look at how lightly Paul holds on to his earthly life in Phil. 1:21-24: "For to me, living is Christ and dying is gain. If I am to live in the flesh, that means fruitful labor for me; and I do not know which I prefer. I am hard pressed between the two: my desire is to depart and be with Christ, for that is far better; but to remain in the flesh is more necessary for you" (NIB). Paul has work to do here, but he never loses sight that heaven is the goal.

In his book on heaven, Randy Alcorn writes,

> Life on Earth matters not because it's the only life we have, but precisely because it isn't—it's the beginning of a life that will continue without end. It's the precursor of life on the New Earth. Eternal life doesn't begin when we die—it has already begun. . . . Understanding Heaven doesn't just tell us *what* to do, but *why*. What God tells us about our future lives enables us to interpret our past and serve him in our present.[1]

If our eyes are really on heaven, then will we really want to put all our energy and affection on accumulating things we're soon going to toss aside anyway—wealth, status, fame, power? Or instead, will we turn our attention to things that last? As Jesus said, "Do not store up for yourselves treasures on earth, where moth and rust consume and where thieves break in and steal; but store up for yourselves treasures in heaven, where neither moth nor rust consumes and where thieves do not break in and steal. For where your treasure is, there your heart will be also" (Matt. 6:19-21, NIB).

- **Concentrating on heaven reminds us that suffering is temporary. Whatever frustrations and hardships we now have to endure will soon be swept away, so we should be filled with optimism and hope.**

Think of all the painful things of life that are more bearable because we know they're only temporary. Imagine, for example, living in a world in which the pain of childbirth was a *permanent* condition for any woman who chose to have a baby. Labor pains would last not just hours but months and years. How many women would be willing to endure that? Yet in our world, because women know that birth pains last only for a relatively short time and then are gone, they're willing to put up with pain for the joy of motherhood.

If heaven is at the forefront of our thinking, then the suffering we endure in this life, though it may be so agonizing that it pushes us to the breaking point, is bearable because we know it will soon be over and will be replaced by something infinitely better.

If heaven is not in our thinking, and even for many Christians it's really not much more than a vague concept, then we're stuck with only what we have here. We have to make sense of a world in which pain will never be eliminated. We have to put our hope in a world in which unfairness and injustice will never be wiped away. To have hope only in this world is to have no hope at all. Alcorn describes the futility of those whose optimism lies only in this world:

> Secular optimists are wishful thinkers. Discovering the present payoffs of optimism, they conduct seminars and write books on thinking positively. Sometimes they capitalize on optimism by becoming rich and famous. But then what happens? They eventually get old or sick, and when they die they go to Hell forever. Their optimism is an illusion, for it fails to take eternity into account.[2]

By contrast, Scripture describes an optimism based on a much broader perspective, in which what happens after death is just as alive in our thinking as the life we're living now:

> So we do not lose heart. Even though our outer nature is wasting away, our inner nature is being renewed day by day. For this slight momentary affliction is preparing us for an eternal weight of glory beyond all measure, because we look not at what can be seen but at what cannot be seen; for what can be seen is temporary, but what cannot be seen

is eternal. For we know that if the earthly tent we live in is destroyed, we have a building from God, a house not made with hands, eternal in the heavens (2 Cor. 4:16—5:1, NIB).

What Paul calls a "slight momentary affliction" will certainly not feel "slight" or "momentary" while we're going through it, of course. It's only by setting it beside the much greater promise of eternity that we can call it "slight" by comparison. Elsewhere, in Romans, he puts it this way: "I consider that the sufferings of this present time are not worth comparing with the glory about to be revealed to us" (Rom. 8:18, NIB). Even when our pain is so deep and bewildering that it is beyond our capacity to sort it out, the Holy Spirit steps in to help us: "Likewise the Spirit helps us in our weakness; for we do not know how to pray as we ought, but that very Spirit intercedes with sighs too deep for words" (Rom. 8:26, NIB).

- **Because it is so easy to let our focus drift away from how our current lives are connected to eternity, we need to constantly remind and encourage each other about the long-term hope we Christians have.**

Whenever I speak words of support to my brothers and sisters in Christ who are going through tough times, I'm sorry to admit that I rarely mention the promise of heaven or the promise of Jesus' return as part of that encouragement. Why don't I? I think the main reason is that such hope seems too far away. Instead, I'm searching for something that will help someone *now*.

In contrast, the early Christians lived in the *constant awareness* that Christ could return at any moment, or that God could take them to heaven at any time. In his introduction to Paul's two letters to the Thessalonians, Peterson writes, "From the day Jesus ascended into heaven, His followers lived in expectancy of His return. He told them He was coming back. They believed He was coming back. They continue to believe it. For Christians, it is the most important thing to know and believe about the future."[3]

Early Christians not only *believed* in Christ's return, but they kept it at the forefront of their communication with one another. After describing some details of the Lord's return in 1 Thess. 4, Paul ends the passage with "Therefore encourage one another with these words" (v. 18, NIB). He follows this with more discussion of the timing of Christ's return, and then he repeats his admonition: "Therefore encourage one another and build each other up, as indeed you are doing" (1 Thess. 5:11, NIB).

Peter also begins his first letter by encouraging his readers with the fact that heaven is a current reality that will help us through the hard times. He writes, "Because Jesus was raised from the dead, we've been given a brand-new life and have everything to live for, including a future in heaven—and the future starts now! God is keeping careful watch over us and the future. The Day is coming when you'll have it all—life healed and whole" (1 Pet. 1:3-5, TM).

Heaven is the prize that will finally reveal that all our waiting has been worth it. Peter ends his letter with the same idea: "The suffering won't last forever. It won't be long before this generous God who has great plans for us in Christ—eternal and glorious plans they are!—will have you put together and on your feet for good. He gets the last word; yes, he does" (1 Pet. 5:10-11, TM).

Questions for Reflection

1. Do you agree with this chapter's point that most Christians today do not make eternity as much a part of their everyday lives as early Christians did? If you agree, why do you think that is?

2. Paul wrote that he did not know which to prefer, remain-

ing in this life or going to be with Christ. Do most Christians today struggle with that choice, or are we more likely to want to cling tenaciously to our present life at all costs?

3. Paul tells the Thessalonian Christians to "encourage one another" by continuing to remind each other of the coming return of Jesus Christ. How often do we encourage each other with that message? What are some ways we could do a better job of that?

4. Does the promise of heaven change your perspective on any of the difficulties you're enduring right now? In what ways?

NOTES

Invitation to the Reader

1. Carl Honore, *In Praise of Slowness: How a Worldwide Movement Is Challenging the Cult of Speed* (San Francisco: HarperSanFrancisco, 2004), 3.

2. Ibid., 12-13.

Introduction

1. Randy Alcorn, *Heaven* (Wheaton, Ill.: Tyndale House Publishers, 2004), 34.

2. Andy Stanley, *Visioneering* (Sisters, Oreg.: Multnomah Press, 1999), 13.

Chapter 1

1. Robert Alter, *The Five Books of Moses: A Translation with Commentary* (New York: W. W. Norton, 2004), xiii.

2. Ibid., 206.

Chapter 2

1. Martin Buber, *Moses: The Revelation and the Covenant* (New York: Harper, 1958), 37.

2. Ibid., 38.

3. John J. Davis, *Moses and the Gods of Egypt: Studies in Exodus* (Grand Rapids: Baker Books, 1986), 65.

Chapter 3

1. Barbara Ehrenreich, *Nickel and Dimed: On (Not) Getting By in America* (New York: Metropolitan Books, 2001), 8.

2. Davis, *Moses and the Gods of Egypt*, 68.

3. Alter, *The Five Books of Moses*, 320.

Chapter 4

1. Jeffrey Kluger, "Secrets of the Shy," *Time*, April 4, 2005, 51-52.

Chapter 5

1. Alter, *The Five Books of Moses*, 341.

2. Eugene H. Peterson, *The Message: The Bible in Contemporary Language* (Colorado Springs: NavPress, 2002), 1342.

Chapter 6

1. Alter, *The Five Books of Moses*, 361.

Chapter 7

1. Claudia Wallis, "The New Science of Happiness," *Time*, January 17, 2005, A8.

2. Ibid.

3. Ibid.

4. Ibid., A9.

5. John I. Durham, *Understanding the Basic Themes of Exodus* (Dallas: Word Publishing, 1990), 104-105.

6. Alter, *The Five Books of Moses*, xiii.

Chapter 8
1. Alter, *The Five Books of Moses*, 388.

Chapter 9
1. Durham, *Understanding the Basic Themes of Exodus*, 74.

Chapter 10
1. Alter, *The Five Books of Moses*, 131.
2. Ibid., 495.

Chapter 11
1. Honore, *In Praise of Slowness*, 2-3.
2. Ibid., 3.
3. Martin Miller, "Wait Watchers," *Los Angeles Times*, December 29, 2004, E1.
4. Ibid.
5. Ibid, E12.
6. Ibid.
7. Honore, *In Praise of Slowness*, 4.
8. Ibid., 49.
9. Stuart McCready, *The Discovery of Time* (Naperville, Ill.: Sourcebooks, 2001), 10.
10. Honore, *In Praise of Slowness*, 34.
11. McCready, *The Discovery of Time*, 4.
12. Ibid., 13.
13. Curt Suplee, "The Sun: Living with a Stormy Star," *National Geographic*, July 2004, 17.
14. Janet Wilson, "Greatest Show on Girth," *Los Angeles Times*, September 20, 2004, A12.

Chapter 12
1. Robert Bly, "Driving Late to Town to Mail a Letter," in *An Introduction to Poetry*, 7th ed., ed. X. J. Kennedy (Glenview, Ill.: Scott, Foresman/Little, Brown, 1990), 85.
2. Sonya Yee, "Bucking a Trend, Austrians Prefer Coffee Their Way," *Los Angeles Times*, December 27, 2004, A11.
3. Ibid.
4. Merle Rubin, "Resisting the Tug of a Fast Life," review of Carl Honore, *In Praise of Slowness: How a Worldwide Movement Is Changing the Cult of Speed in Los Angeles Times Book Review*, May 23, 2004, R7.

Chapter 13
1. Tim Layden, "Youth was served at the birthplace of the Games as 22-year-old Justin Gatlin prevailed in one of the swiftest 100-meter dashes in history," *Sports Illustrated*, August 30, 2004, <http://proquest.umi.com.pq.resources.apu.edu/pqdweb?did=687576181&sid=1&Fmt=3&clientid=23686&RQT=309&VName=PQD>.

Chapter 15
1. Alcorn, *Heaven*, 443.
2. Ibid., 443-44.
3. Peterson, *The Message*, 2151.

ACKNOWLEDGMENTS

I could not have written this book without the help of many people. I wish to thank the Beacon Hill Press staff, especially Bonnie Perry and Judi Perry, who believed in this book from the beginning. I am grateful for the work of Barry Russell, Jennifer Prentice, and Jonathan Wright. I would also like to thank my agent, Steve Laube, who was a great source of help and encouragement.

As I wrote this book, I taught the material to the Genesis Sunday School class at First Church of the Nazarene in Pasadena, California. The following class members were particularly helpful and encouraging as the book took shape: Daniel and Perla Dreibus, Craig Foreman, Brian and Maria Garvin, Dorene Lee, Janet Lindsey, Daniel McKinney, Marion Oppenheim, Mat and Edie Roberts, Beth Sarkar, Debbie and Mike Archer, Astrid Shah, David Silvey, and Steve and Deniece Zwick.

I would especially like to thank Carolyn Dunlop-Brace and Laura and Roger Conover, who helped with some specific content in the book.

The Ninos, a group of Christian artists and writers to which I belong, prayed for this book and gave me constant encouragement. I would especially like to thank Tom Allbaugh, Diana Glyer, Mike Glyer, Lynn Maudlin, Teresa Johnston, Tim Davis, Kayla Winiarz, Liz Leahy, Monica Ganas, Lois Carlson, and Adrien Lowery.

My colleagues at Azusa Pacific University have been especially supportive of my work on this book. I wish to thank Marsha Fowler, who taught two faith integration courses, sponsored by a grant from the Lilly Endowment, that I took during the writing of this book. My friends in the second of those courses gave helpful feedback during my research: Carole Lambert, Charity Plaxton-Hennings, Curtis Hsia, Beth Houskamp, and Theresa Tisdale. I would also like to thank Azusa's provost, Michael Whyte, who has been particularly supportive of my writing endeavors. I would also like to thank James Hedges, David Esselstrom, David Weeks, Sue Ney, Diane Guido, Bev Stanford, and Glenys Gee.

Finally, this book would not have been possible without the love, support, and patience of my wife, Peggy, and my children, Jacob and Katie.

For more information, or to contact the author, please visit www.josephbentz.com